VIRUS

*Spread the good news
about your company
via The Human Factor*

Dale

You can accomplish
anything you set
your mind to

Congrats on
graduation &
starting this new
chapter in your
life!

REBECCA D. TURNER

Cover and book design: www.EssexGraphix.com
Editor: Tana Grubb (tanagrubb@hotmail.com)

Trafford Publishing
6E - 2333 Government Street
Victoria, BC, Canada V8T 4P4

www.readvirus.com

ISBN: 978-1-4251-7298-5

Printed in the United States of America

TABLE OF CONTENTS

MAKE BELIEVE

"Many aspects of history are unanticipated and unforeseen, predictable only in retrospect: the fall of the Berlin Wall is a single recent example. Yet in one vital area, the emergence and spread of new infectious diseases, we can already predict the future—and it is threatening and dangerous to us all."

—Laurie Garrett
The Coming Plague

"What I feel is whatever I might imagine is probably right round the corner anyway. So many things that were fiction fifteen years ago are now taking place."

—Michael Crichton
During an interview about his book *Next* when asked "Is there anything in your book that you would like to be real?"

"Imagination is everything. It is a preview of life's coming attractions."
—Albert Einstein (1879-1955)
Nobel prize winning theoretical physicist

Ah... make believe. What did you pretend to be or do in your childhood? For my younger brother and me, it was anything goes. With my creativity and his willingness to do just about anything, we often horrified our mom.

One favorite make believe included a fuzzy, pink toilet seat cover that created a stylish and very '80s rock and roll head of hair. White Snake, Quiet Riot, Poison, and KISS had nothing on my brother's hair.

A clothesline strung across the basement ceiling with clothes pinned together made our "stage." We were ready for a concert—a one-man act with a trap set and the most amazingly talented percussionist the world had ever seen. I of course was one-heck-of-a stage manager. The bands I recently mentioned? Well, they were our opening acts! From our basement with cement floors and walls and no windows, my brother and I toured the world.

I hope that story recalled a fond memory of playing as a child, and how much fun it was to pretend... to make believe.

But, at some point we must enter adulthood. Many of us lose the uninhibited freedom to play. This is too bad because play and recreation are what we often need in our businesses to be creative and keep renewing what we provide to our customers. As our customers change what is important to them, we have to listen to them and remain open to new ideas. To progress and be a leader in our industry, we have to rethink what we do and think outside-the-box to differentiate ourselves from our competition.

BRAINSTORMING

As adults, to encourage out-of-the-box thinking and good creative ideas to enhance the growth of our business or other pursuits, we frame our creative meetings around a creative thinking technique called brainstorming. It is the spontaneous contribution of ideas from all members of a group so that creative ideas (similar to those we had as children) can flow easily without the fear of ridicule or rejection. Practically anything goes during brainstorming.

Why are books like *Tipping Point, Freakonomics* and *The World is Flat* so wildly popular? I believe somewhere in our stuffy business lives we are ready to take a fresh new creative look at everything. Unless we live in a creative field of business like marketing, most of us live out of one side of our brain—the analytical. As an avid reader of business books I can tell you that many of the authors write to us out of the analytical side of our brain as well. So if you are used to that kind of business book, this will be a different journey for you. But because it is different, it may just give you exactly what you need to ignite your business.

As you read this book, I believe you will find analogies that apply to your businesses and just like the examples in this book, you too will prosper because you value The Human Factor.

So play along with me. The following scenario is fictional but please read it with an open mind.

NOW PRETEND IT IS 2060...

Rising malpractice insurance for physicians and skyrocketing health care costs had almost bankrupted the United States. In the United States, health care spending and benefits had gotten to a point that only the very wealthy could pay for private care. Desperate for a solution, the government turned toward corporate giant Walco for an answer. In response, Walco had put together a task force of some of the brightest minds in the world to come up with a plan that would put the much needed health care in place. Walco was the largest corporation in the world based in the United States and had accumulated the financial means to put together a task force to design a better health care management system.

TARNISHED REPUTATION

The United States' reputation had become tarnished worldwide. With Walco being based in the United States and creating what would become virtually a fix to the world health care crisis, the United States' reputation would be restored both innovatively and politically.

Because Walco already had stores strategically located in every major city around the world and even in many of the smaller towns in the United States, it provided the perfect blueprint for the start of the new health care system. The company already had pharmacies for dispensing prescriptions and other health care products. With the implementation of a new body scan machine at each location, Walco stores were ideal for the new health management system.

HAD BECOME VERY GRAY

Once the new plan was implemented, the line between the United States government and Walco became very gray. Every major country had a distribution center (DC) that was the hub for distributing pharmaceuticals, health care products, gene therapy, and medical treatment plans. Smaller countries were assigned to the closest DC. These DCs were equipped with the new body scanning devices so that individuals could go to a center, have a complete body scan and a diagnosis and treatment plan within minutes. If the treatment plan called for invasive surgery, the patient received a list of referral surgeons. Prescriptions were filled automatically within minutes and at the pharmacy ready for pick up.

GENOMETERS AND NANOMETERS

The Genometer and Nanometer machines were located at the DCs as well. The injection of the right genes to cure diseases was more streamlined with the scanners being able to pinpoint what gene therapy was needed to cure multiple diseases. The injection of nanos into the body to search and find the abnormal cells was a breakthrough treatment to cure cancer. The nanos were trained to search inside the body for the abnormal cells and attach to them. The patient could then walk through a magnetic field and the nanos would explode taking the abnormal cancerous cells with them. With the body scan equipment, genometer, and nanometers, the DCs were a full service health care facility for all non-invasive treatments.

THE LIFE OF A BODY SCAN TECHNICIAN

The health care part of the distribution centers was regulated and mandated by the United States government. Some of the more developed countries had what were called private physician medical centers (PMCs) which were very expensive. Only the very wealthy were able to use them and all diagnoses, procedures, pharmaceuticals, and treatments were on a cash basis. Unless patients were going to pay cash for medical treatment and visit a private medical center, which was very expensive and few could afford, patients had to visit a DC for diagnosis before any treatment could be given. Eighty percent of the world's population relied on the DCs for health care. When surgery was required and recommended, the physicians and surgeons patients were referred to were employees of the United States government.

Seth Daniels was one of the technicians Walco trained and hired. His compensation came partly from Walco and partly from the United States government. On average, Seth would spend two to three days at a distribution center testing and retesting the body scanners to make sure they were working properly. Then he would be off to the next center driving or flying depending on the location. His schedule would take him literally around the world in eleven months. He would then have one month off. His grueling schedule would begin again each January.

HANDSOME LIVING

Technicians like Seth made a very handsome living. Their compensation from the government as an employee was about equal to what Walco paid them in the form of contract labor. Seth's 2059 gross income was just over one million. Seth's routine consisted of arriving in the city with a distribution center. He would first check himself in online to notify the hotel that he was in town and would be staying at his reserved accommodations for that night. He would then go to

5

meet with the manager of the Walco distribution center, along with several of the management team members. Normally the meeting would last three to four hours recapping the prior year's service at the DC, any troubleshooting needed, and any changes that staff were to report for the current year and going forward. Depending on the size of the DC there might be fifteen to twenty people who would attend.

LUCRATIVE BUSINESS

Because the body scanners and health care side of Walco's distribution centers were such a lucrative part of Walco's business, a few of the management team would make sure that Seth and technicians like him were treated to three meals a day often at the finest restaurants in the area. Several of the key managers would join the staff at these meals, which were often an extension of a prior meeting or discussion during the day. The grueling schedule that these technicians had eleven months out of the year left little time for a personal and social life. It is no wonder that Seth became very close to the people in these various countries that he spent a good amount of time with each year. After his tenure as a technician, some of them had really become his friends.

It had been nine months since Seth had to make the long trek from New York to India. But to do business with the largest retailer in the world, Walco, one made sacrifices. Little did Seth know what this particular trip would bring not only to him but to the beginning of a chain of events that would affect the rest of the world.

03.01.2060

March for Seth meant Iraq, Iran, Afghanistan, and Pakistan. During the yearly briefing in January, Seth met with George Jones of the World Health Organization (WHO). George had told Seth to keep an eye out for anything that might be out of the ordinary and to report back what he saw. There had been reports of very critically ill patients dying for no apparent or explained reason and many were dying from something other than what their complaint was when they had been admitted.

A FULL PLATE

Seth's plate was already full and this added reporting requirement would extend his stay in each DC three to four hours. But it was obvious George wasn't asking him, he was telling him. In fact, all body scan technicians were required to take on this extra task if they wanted to keep their jobs.

Besides, Seth would report into a digital recorder that would be sent electronically to George in Washington, D.C., so it wouldn't be so bad, Seth thought.

GROSSLY OVERCROWDED

The government had other concerns. The health physician centers were grossly overcrowded, with most patient rooms doubled up with four patients in each room. The government would have to spend money to build additional rooms. Discussions on Capitol Hill focused on where to get the funding for the much-needed expansions. The president had appointed a team, which included George Jones, to research just how many extra beds were needed and to project out the cost of increasing the size of the centers.

INFECTION RATES START TO DOUBLE

As the reports came in from the body scan technicians, the disease did seem to take only the sick or elderly and many already dying. The details were not entirely clear as many reports stated the cause of death was unknown, but it appeared that what these individuals were dying from was not what they initially were brought in for. In the beginning, the rate as far as the U.S. government could tell was about one percent of the patients at the health care centers. Within six months as the technicians continued to report what they saw, the rate had doubled to two percent. Ninety days later the rate doubled again to four percent. Twelve months from the first recorded death, the rate doubled again to eight percent. So George wasn't surprised when the technicians reported to him after eleven months that the rate had grown to ten percent.

A BRIGHT SPOT

George and his team had been projecting out the twenty year growth plan needed for the health physician centers. As fast as the death rate was increasing, George and his team reported the numbers to the president. They were able to project a decrease in expansion for the centers from what they had presented to him just twelve months before.

Ironically, this actually turned out to be a bright spot in the report, as the government could actually project a decrease in the need for funding to expand the health physician centers.

Clearly, every country on the globe had been affected by the virus.

WHERE TO START

With the passage of time and the increase in travel, it was becoming more and more difficult for the Center for Disease Control and Prevention (CDC) to pinpoint exactly where a microbe first emerged. The human immunodeficiency virus (HIV or AIDS {Acquired Immunodeficiency Syndrome}) was a classic case in point as it surfaced simultaneously on three continents and spread swiftly around the globe.

A change in the interaction between the agent or virus, the host, and the environment is usually required for an epidemic to develop. Populations and their migration are considered in attempts to understand the changing patterns of diseases. Could the virus evolve and have the ability to infect macrophages in the lungs and thus, become a respiratory disease? The medical field now recognizes that RNA viruses will continue to evolve rapidly as they have over the millennia. As the epidemic of AIDS made clear, pathogens can and will arise. It was important to know how exactly, viruses gained entry into the human body via alveoli in the lungs viral activity. In the real world, viral mutants had to deliver their genetic payloads to the proper types of cells inside an animal or person in order to cause disease. Only recently had science started to discover the discipline of microbial ecology dedicated to studies of the behavior of microbes inside the human body.

LESS THAN 0.64 MICRON

Just under one one-hundred-thousandth of an inch was all the distance that separated the air environment in the lungs from the human bloodstream.

That was all the new strain seemed to need to attack, usually only the weak with low immune systems. For many of these people, it wasn't a matter of if they would die, but when.

What chilled Eric Lerner of the CDC wasn't the ability of the virus to cause death within weeks, but the mode of transmission: the virus was airborne.

Every human interaction, every handshake as part of business etiquette, so much as a breath or sigh directed at another during a business meeting or lunch was a potential environment for further spread of the disease.

As the horror of this disease unfolded, some members of the CDC had read the historical account of how the AIDS disease had spread throughout the world decades before. The United States government and health officials had continued to ignore what they did not understand and did not want to believe until the disease was triumphant enough, based on the thousands of lives it took. Then and only then did the government and officials take notice. At the first outbreak of AIDS, it seemed to only take one segment of society: gay men. At the time, it seemed easy to ignore, and turn our backs on this segment of society.

Lerner realized that history often repeats itself. But when it comes to people, humanness or lack thereof, he had always hoped that we've learned from our past mistakes as a society. But this time, we use excuses like rising health care costs, inadequate health care facilities, and a grossly overpopulated planet, so we can sleep better at night. Eric Lerner thought to himself, we pathetically turn our heads the other way while the disease continues to ravage its way through its victims.

After all, Lerner thought, we tell ourselves, nature takes care of the inefficiencies of human nature: survival of the fittest, so to speak, to defend our irresponsible actions.

So once again, Lerner contemplated, we fall prey to mistakes of the past. This time we turn our backs on a different segment of society, our sick and elderly.

EXHAUSTING CAREER?

As Seth was finishing his last month in Australia, New Zealand, and Mexico, he couldn't help but think to himself, could adding three to four hours to each visit cause me to be so much more tired? Or was he just getting older? Maybe he just didn't have the energy anymore for this kind of grueling schedule. He noticed the new technicians being hired were at least ten years his junior, maybe more. Could it be that at age thirty-five he would be replaced? He worked hard at staying in shape and he knew that was key to continuing the pace of his job. In fact, he kept himself in such good shape it was common for people to mistake his age by ten years or more.

MARIA VALDEZ

One of the managers of the distribution centers in Mexico, his last stop before returning to the U.S., was Maria Valdez. Now that was someone Seth always looked forward to visiting. Maria was Seth's dream of the perfect woman. Beautiful beyond words, inside and out, but she acted as if she had no clue as to how perfect she really was. She was an intelligent, independent business woman with the smarts to do anything she set her mind to. Her great looks and confidence didn't hurt her chances of being unstoppable in any endeavor she chose. She was humble and modest with an obvious love for her country and her people. Three years ago when Seth first met her, she had taken over one of the poorest run DCs and turned it around in three short years into one of the most profitable and best run facilities Seth had encountered.

Because of Maria's success, she could literally have the facility of her choosing to manage. But, she chose to stay, for less pay, to be with her people in her country. Seth thought her obvious love for both her people and her country was admirable.

If only he could stay an extra few days, get to know her and share with her how he felt about her. There was just no time and this being his last stop, he was exhausted.

Maybe after a few more years with his handsome salary, he could put enough away to feel secure and take a lower paying job that wouldn't take him away from a home and a family eleven months of the year. Maybe he could find someone, maybe Maria, and start the family he had always longed for.

On Seth's last visit, during a casual business dinner, he had reached across the table and brushed Maria's arm. They had caught each other's glance, and, for a moment Seth had wondered if she might think of him the way he thought of her. They had both smiled and laughed to break the awkwardness. Now a year later, seeing Maria again brought back those familiar feelings. "Ridiculous," Seth told himself. "I barely know her."

What made it even more odd was no matter how painful it was to know he couldn't touch her like he wanted, he would still choose to be in a room with her over anyone else in his life in the world. She was so wonderful to be around, like a breathe of fresh air, and the room always filled with positive vibrant energy when she appeared. So yes, he would rather be in her presence than not, no matter how painful it was.

A DEAL WITH THE DEVIL

When Seth had become a technician ten years ago, he knew it would be a lonely road. But in 2050, how many twenty-five-year olds had the opportunity to make eight hundred and twenty thousand dollars a year, and enjoy the excitement of traveling the world? Who in their right mind would have passed that up? But now, Seth thought it felt more like he had made a deal with the devil ten years ago. He had nowhere to go to even make half his current income. If he could hang on for just a few more years…

01.01.2061

By the time authorities were starting to take action to combat the disease, Seth had already been hospitalized and given less than a year to live. Because of the mobility of the body scan technicians, Seth wasn't alone. A high percentage of the technicians were either dead or dying. Thus far, death was the only known result for anyone who contacted the virus.

The number of reported deaths worldwide was just twenty thousand less than the number of deaths previously caused by AIDS, after society had finally acted to control the disease. Besides being airborne, the critical difference in AIDS and this virus was how quickly the virus took over the body and the certainty of death once infected.

The task force of the United States government, the World

Health Organization, and the CDC put together a plan of action to first curtail the disease and then appoint specialists to study it in hopes of eradicating it.

The government's reputation had suffered over the last several decades, and could not take the risk politically of not appearing to be on the cutting edge of this disease.

EXCEPTIONS WERE MADE

Since Walco had the patent on the lucrative body scanners, they would not let the technical applications of the scanners be known to anyone except the technicians that they hired and trained. Although most patents would have run out, because of Walco's position with the United States government, exceptions were made to extend the patent on the scanners. Previously this served Walco well as they had 100 percent of the market of the WHO via their patented scanners. Now, however, it was coming back to haunt them as with no one available to fix the scanners, this once lucrative business was near extinction.

The world was dangerously close to going back to more primitive health care as the shortage of the body scan technicians left the scanners around the world in dire need of repair with no realistic estimated time of recovery. The managers of the centers knew once they were down, the odds of actually finding a technician healthy, alive and willing to take the risk of world travel, would be a true rarity. The reality was that 80 percent of the population that relied on the DCs for health care were on their own. The world, for the time being anyway, closed the door on a health care system that had worked beautifully for the last fifty years.

The frenzied media around the world covered the "end of world" ideologies. The United States and the rest of the world contemplated what kind of world was in store for all.

02.01.2061

A month had passed.

The task force finally had statistics on the rate the disease was spreading. As the stats were distributed to each member, the room fell silent. The ramifications of the news began to sink in, and no one had to say what was on all of their minds. Just how far would this thing spread...

NOW IMAGINE...

Every interaction handshake encounter is telling another about your business. Your business can spread as easily as a virus. No marketing money spent, it effortlessly spreads via word-of-mouth and the connectivity of people. You have created a business experience for your customer. Just like the horrific virus in the story, your customers would know about your business's reputation before they encountered your business. You are so well-known for how you treat your employees and your customers and how you give back to humanity, that your reputation precedes the encounter with your next customer.

This is what I call The Human Factor, how you treat your employees and your customers and how you give back to humanity. You do well by doing good. People want to do business with you and they passionately want everyone else they know to do business with you as well because of what you stand for.

This becomes your marketing. You show you care by these three aspects. This causes your customers to care and to take the time to make sure everyone in their world is doing business with you too.

This book is about how other companies have used The Human Factor to grow and market their businesses and how you can take the attributes and apply them to your business to grow and market it as well.

Introduction:
"Ring Around the Rosy"

"Man's mind stretched to a new idea, never goes back to its original dimension."

—Oliver Wendell Holmes (1809-1894)

Physician and one of the best regarded American poets

"If we know where we are and something about how we got there, we might see where we are trending, and if the outcomes which lie naturally in our course are unacceptable, make timely change."

—Abraham Lincoln (1809-1865)

16th president of the United States

EVERYONE I'VE EVER ASKED...

I have a very important question to ask you. When you were growing up, no matter where you lived, did you play the game "Ring around the Rosy?" If you have children, have you played it with them? I'm pretty sure I know the answer. As I was researching my first book *Tattoo* and as I have done speaking engagements centered around that book, I have asked people the same question. I have never seen a blank stare, a confused look or a comment like, "I don't know what you are talking about." Virtually everyone I've ever asked has played this game.

I have spoken at events in Las Vegas, New York City and throughout the Dallas Fort Worth metroplex and polled over 2,000 people. I have asked a full-blooded Hawaiian woman, a man from Milwaukee, Wisconsin, a lady from New York City, two men from Zambia in Africa, a man from Mexico City, and two women from Brazil. They all played this game.

To further illustrate my point, the origin of the game and the words of the nursery rhyme are relevant to why, for the most part, all of us have played the game.

Can you remember the words? Close your eyes, imagine where you were when you played this game (a backyard, a basement, maybe at your swimming lessons) and state the words out loud:

Ring around the rosy, pocket full of posies, ashes, ashes, we all fall down.

Now, do you know what the lines to the rhyme mean? As I do my speaking engagements, a few people know about the origin and what possibly one line means, but rarely do they know the entire history. So here you go...

660 YEARS AGO

Six hundred and sixty years ago a plague wiped out one-third of Europe's population. Twenty-five million people died of the Bubonic plague, also known as the black death, between 1347 and 1350. Thus is the story of "Ring around the Rosy."

Originally, the words were "ring-a-ring o'roses" referring to the red rash that people would get once they had the disease. "A pocket full of posies" referred to the superstition that putting rose petals in a pocket would ward off the evil spirits that carried the plague. "A-tishoo! A-tishoo!" imitated the constant sneezing associated with those afflicted.

The original "ashes to ashes," changed over time to "ashes, ashes" and described what was done to try and stop the disease from spreading: the bodies were burned. "We all fall down" alludes to what would most likely happen to those afflicted: death.

Because 85 percent of those afflicted with the disease would die, to try and curtail the plague, once authorities knew someone in that family had the disease, the door of the home was locked... from the outside. After sufficient time had passed and all in the home were presumed dead from the disease, authorities would reopen the home and drag the bodies into the street to burn them in hopes of stopping the plague.

According to history, people in their villages would gather frequently in the streets and dance hysterically in anticipation of "tomorrow we die."

It is believed that this frantic dancing relieved the people's anxiety. This dancing and singing continued long after the plague was over, but the adults no longer participated. Only the children continued singing the words and dancing and eventually created a rhyme out of the original version.

AS A NURSERY RHYME

The "song" as a nursery rhyme first appeared in Kate Greenaway's *Mother Goose*, in 1881. Isn't it interesting that 660 years later, we can walk by a playground and hear children singing this song? How did this happen? By word-of-mouth, by being passed down from children through the years, and the contagious connectivity of people. It was a very trying and emotional time for the people of London. The rhyme exemplifies the power of word-of-mouth, the power of people, and the ability we have through words as a society to invoke change.

Isn't it amazing that marketers spend millions of dollars a year trying to get us to pay attention and remember their message just until our next trip to the store? This message has lasted over 600 years with no marketing dollars behind it and it is still alive and well today.

WHAT DOES THIS HAVE TO DO WITH MARKETING MY BUSINESS?

I know this is a very morbid story and I am always a little surprised as I do speaking engagements how few people know about where the story originated and what it means. But when I ask them to close their eyes and recall the rhyme, they not only recite it (exactly as I have described) word for word, but more often than not they chant them back to me. This is very compelling in a room with several hundred people in it. That being said, when I ask people from all over the country, it appears that we have all sung the rhyme at one time in our lives. I'm going to bet that you did, didn't you?

WE NEED TO GET THEIR ATTENTION

I am going to bet that you will never think about "Ring around the Rosy" quite the same ever again. And just like that nursery rhyme, I want you to forever think differently about how you market your business. I know you are like me, your life is crazy and you are constantly on the move (and I'll bet that you and I won't slow down anytime in the near future).

Researcher's tell us that we remember very little of what we read and hear today. As you try to get your message across to your students, your customers, your readership, and your audience whatever it may be, it is harder and harder to get people interested and, more importantly, to remember your company or message and what you have to say or offer them.

People at my presentations tell me they will never think of "Ring around the Rosy" the same way ever again. So too it is my job to have you never think about marketing your business the same way again either.

Your clients and customers need what you have whether it is a message, a product or a service. You know they do and you can do it better than your competition. You wouldn't be reading this book about how to grow your business if you weren't already good in some respect and always looking to improve. Being open to change and to improving how you do business is a true sign that you are already and will continue to be successful. We have to continually change how we reach our customers to stay ahead of our competition. Your message needs to be heard and your customers need to be doing business with you. You must first get their attention, then get them to care. So just like you in your business, I needed to get your attention. I needed to get you to pick up this book so that you can benefit from the message it has for you to improve your life.

I think I have succeeded in getting your attention. My ego would like to think you'd remember every word I have written. But I am a realist and my life is very similar to yours in the challenges we have to get people to listen to our message, buy our product, and remember us when they need our products or services again.

So years from now, you will forget many things you have read, but I would bet that one year, five years, or even ten years from now, you will remember the "Ring Around the Rosy" story. You may even remember many of the gory details, but better yet, you will remember why the story is at the heart of spreading your message or your service.

If you do, then one of my goals for you has been reached. Now that I have your attention, throughout the remainder of this book, my goal is to express to you why that story has everything to do with how you market your business today.

AN EXPERIENCE WE HAVE TOGETHER

I don't want this just to be a book that you read. This is an experience that we will share together, as you learn what it takes to develop your own Human Factor (more on this in a moment) and use it to spread the great news about your company.

I believe that if you are reading this book, you are a relatively disciplined person so I'm going to let you in on a secret in this book and what will be part of this amazing experience. There is a surprise at the end. But please don't flip to the end: you'll ruin the surprise and you won't get as much out of this book if you do. Read each chapter. Apply what will work for you to your business. At the end, you will be glad you waited.

Virus is full of stories and examples that are a testament to the connectivity of people, their relationships, and the contagious way our businesses can spread around the world. Through case examples and interviews, you will understand why this "story" is essential for you to grow your businesses today.

There is human value to all aspects of business including employees, customers, the business networks that we create either to expand our business or increase the knowledge base for our business, and those mentors or think tanks that helped us and continue to help us along the way. There is human value in what we give back to humanity from what our businesses create. As consumers we vote with our checkbooks when we have a choice, to do business with companies that value the human side of business—how they treat their employees via benefits, pay and general fairness. We have the chance to vote with our voice by speaking out against companies who don't show they value The Human Factor in business.

BUY LOCAL

When possible, I believe we need to patronize local businesses and support them when we purchase goods and services. As you and I travel across this great country of ours, the towns and cities across our nation are starting to look the same with the same familiar chains in every town we visit, leaving little character or variance to intrigue or inspire us. This is what I call The Human Factor.

THE HUMAN FACTOR

This book is about why today, The Human Factor is more important than ever. And if you and I value and use The Human Factor to grow our businesses, we will not only prosper, we will improve humanity and at the end of the day feel generally good about what we have created.

This may seem a little idealistic to you now, but when you are done with this experience, you will have seen many examples of how very large corporations and small businesses choose to value the human side of business and as a result have prospered because they did so.

"EVERYONE'S DOING BUSINESS WITH CHINA"

After reading this book, if your product or service can be marketed overseas, then my hope is that you will not stop spreading the word of your business at U.S. borders. As in Thomas L. Friedman's book, *The World is Flat*, the world has gotten flatter, and I believe, in a sense, smaller. As evidence, in an interview with Pam Minick of Billy Bob's Texas, the world's largest honky tonk, she said that Billy Bob's was planning to expand into Beijing, China. That stopped me in my tracks. I had generally thought of industries like manufacturing or labor "exporting" to China. But franchising the "world's largest honky tonk" in Beijing? How more western can you get? As I left I thought to myself, "I guess everyone is doing business with China."

So as a business owner or manager, who can have the foresight to grow your company, I want you to think broader, wider and smaller.

To survive in our ever and rapidly changing technologically advanced, fast-paced and flattening world, we will not only need to rely more and more on our human relationships to succeed, we will actually long for it.

Now that you know what The Human Factor is, let's start the journey and see how we can apply The Human Factor attributes to grow your business and at the same time be proud of what you created.

THE HUMAN FACTOR

"You and I are not so different."

—Green Goblin
To Spiderman in *Spiderman II*

"Treat people as if they were what they ought to be and you help them become what they are capable of being."

—Johann Wolfgang von Goethe (1749-1832)
Well-known for his literary works

"In the end, all business operations can be reduced to three words: people, product and profits. People come first. Unless you've got a good team, you can't do much with the other two."

—Lee Iacocca
Well-known American industrialist
and one of the most recognized businessmen in the world

After all, when you break us down to our very core, even though we are as unique as we can be with our own set of DNA and as specific as our individual fingerprints, we share one thing in common, we are human. We sin. We get speeding tickets. We stay too long in a bad relationship. We try not to have to say "I'm sorry." We have hopes and dreams. We are human.

UNDERCOVER WORK

In *Nickel and Dimed, On (Not) Getting By in America*, an amazing book by Barbara Ehrenreich, she describes her experiences at going undercover as a low-wage worker to see if she could make it financially. While having a $30 lunch at a French restaurant with one of the editors she works with, the subject of poverty came up. She and the editor wondered, "How, in particular, we wondered, were the roughly four million women about to be booted into the labor market by welfare reform going to make it on $6 or $7 an hour?" Ehrenreich commented, "Someone ought to do the old-fashioned kind of journalism —you know go out there and try it for themselves." And the rest is history as she delved into manual work to conduct her research.

Ehrenreich has this to say about why minimum wage workers stay at minimum wage and don't advance to other high paying jobs. "My guess is that the indignities imposed on so many low-wage workers—drug tests, the constant surveillance, being "reamed out" by managers—are part of what keeps wages low. If you're made to feel unworthy enough, you may come to think that what you're paid is what you are actually worth. Insofar as the poor have to work near the dwellings of the rich—as in the case of so many service and retail jobs—they are stuck with lengthy commutes or dauntingly expensive housing. This of course makes it even harder for low-wage workers to actually survive. Living paycheck to paycheck would work as long as nothing unexpected happens."

Ph.D. OR NOT

Ehrenreich profoundly notes, "Whatever my accomplishments in the rest of my life, in the low-wage work world I was a person of average ability—capable of learning the job and also capable of screwing up." In fact, she originally worried that she would be "discovered." She really wasn't a low-wage worker, but an accomplished author with twelve books under her belt, three of which have become *New York Times* bestsellers. (Since that is a goal of mine, besides her amazing writing and insight, I was already impressed.) She has a Ph.D. in biology. She thought people in the low-wage work world would see right through her and see how smart she was. Barbara quickly found that was the least of her worries. No one ever questioned that she had always lived as her co-workers who "were just like her" trying to survive in a $6-$7 an hour world. Her biggest challenge became how to survive financially, live in a half-way safe and decent environment, and put up with all of the seemingly unnecessary antics of her supervisors.

MY OWN PERSONAL EXPERIENCE
(BUT FOR THE GRACE OF GOD...)

From my own life experiences and from stories people have told me, I have come to the conclusion that the best opportunity for low-wage workers to advance is if someone along the way gives them a chance to let them try to see if they could do something other than $7 dollar an hour work.

After reading *Nickel and Dimed*, I thought, "But for the grace of God, there go I." When I graduated from college with a B.A. in 1985, I found out just how hard it was to find a job, let alone start a career. Even though I had a college degree, it was tough finding someone to give me a chance. They all wanted experience and being just out of college—I had none. I also had no money. I sent resumes to 75 different companies and started calling them to try to get an interview. Not one of them wanted to talk to me.

A friend of mine's sister in Dallas offered her couch until I got on my feet. I spent a horrid two weeks on that couch. I went to interview after interview, all resulting in the same thing—they wanted experience and I had none to offer. I kept thinking if someone would just give me a chance. I knew I would be good at something. I just had no clue what. In one interview in an intimidating high-rise glass building in Dallas, the man interviewing me chuckled because I had talked his assistant into giving me an interview and told me, "Young lady, I'm sure you will be good at something. Come back when you have some experience." I remember thinking, I guess that was a compliment, but it certainly did not help me get started on my route to actually gaining experience and finding a job.

IN DESPERATION

I worried that I would ever find something. I saw an advertisement for a receptionist at a health club chain and thought, they have to have other positions available, like management. I called and was informed that they did have a management position available but it was in Fort Worth. I had driven directly from Kansas to Dallas and knew nothing about the area. The woman I was staying with and her friends groaned and said that Fort Worth was so small and backwoods. But I knew I had to find something as my pride would not let me go back to Kansas, like my family was trying to get me to do. I felt going back would mean I had failed.

So I interviewed and accepted a job as the manager of a Bally's health club chain called President's in Fort Worth. I was offered $8.50 an hour to manage the club. That was 1986. I remember that even then it was difficult to make it on that income alone. Minimum wage now is $5.85. That is incredible! I made $8.50 over twenty years ago and know it was entry level management, but it was hard to survive on $8.50 then. How can anyone survive on $5.85 an hour now?

AFFORDABLE AND SAFE HOUSING

As I read Ehrenreich's book, and of her search for an affordable apartment in a safe part of town, I had a flashback to my apartment hunting in Fort Worth after I landed my job at the health club. I had decided I could afford $250 a month on rent. I was determined not to spend one dime more. As I searched in the paper, and not knowing the city, I just looked at places that were at that price, no matter where in town they were since I didn't know the town anyway. At that price, I kept finding places in a part of Fort Worth that even today is a very seedy part of town. I remember pulling to the side of the road and crying, thinking I didn't want to live there; it was so ugly and it seemed unsafe. My pride wouldn't let me quit and I finally found a place in west Fort Worth for $250 a month in a much better part of town.

EXTRA PART-TIME WORK

During my year and a half at the health club, I was never really happy with my income. I had two other part-time jobs to supplement my income. I was a waitress, and boy do I feel for waitresses after that! I absolutely hated it, but it was one of the easiest jobs to find. The second job was loading freight for a trucking company. They paid $13.75 an hour and even though it was manual labor, I rationalized that, with my degree, I was at least worth that.

At the trucking company, when you were put on the schedule, it wasn't a guarantee that you would be able to work that day. If you were on the 6 a.m. shift, you had to call in two hours before, at 4 a.m. to see if they needed you. After two weeks of calling and being told they didn't need me, I knew they didn't want to give me a chance. So I called human resources and talked to Les Dixon, the human resources director, who assured me that the next time I called in, there would be a slot for me. Sure enough, the next day I called in, they gave me a chance and let me work.

I was determined to do the best job I could every day I went in and at least make them glad they had given me a chance. A few of the supervisors actually liked my work over the guys. Being small, I could go in the trailer and dig out "hot" freight, freight that was mis-loaded and had to be removed and sent on a plane to reach its destination.

THE ONLY WOMAN

I was the first and only woman that loaded freight and it was hard physical work. I remember being so tired that on my one day off a week, I did little more than sleep.

Les Dixon came through for me again, when he noticed one day on my resume that I had a degree from Kansas State University, also his alma mater. He asked me why I was loading freight when I had a degree. I told him I had not been able to find anything that paid close to $13.75 an hour and I felt I was at least worth that. He suggested I apply to be a dock supervisor which I did several times but was never offered the job. I was eventually told that I didn't understand union workers and had been too friendly with them.

HARASSMENT

As you can probably imagine, I got harassed by some of the guys. Some of them liked me but some took offense as if I were out to prove something. I honestly wasn't there to prove anything. It was just the only place I could find that paid that high a wage for non-skilled labor. I didn't want to make a career of this line of work, and figured someday I would look back on this and smile at the whole experience. In fact, I still have the steel-toed boots we were required to wear. They are in my closet—right next to all my business shoes. They are a reminder of my hard work and my struggle to find my calling in life.

AN INJURY

One day a supervisor, who repeatedly tried to give me work he didn't think I could handle, gave me a job that required me tossing heavy long pieces over my head so they would rest on top of the nearly full trailer. I did want to prove to him that he couldn't give me anything I couldn't handle and that no matter what he did, I wasn't going to quit. I finished the trailer in half the time he allotted and he was shocked. He asked several of the guys if they had helped me. They of course hadn't and the supervisors who liked me laughed at him as he walked all the way back down to the other end of the dock. I may have proven something to him, but that repeated movement was more than my body could handle and I hurt my traps, the trapezius muscles between your shoulder and your neck. The next morning I could barely lift my head off of my pillow.

CAME TO MY SENSES

It took that injury, not being able to move for a few days and the doctor telling me to not lift for two weeks, to make me realize I couldn't keep this up. So I called Les and he made good on his promise of finding me an office job. I manually calculated time cards for payroll and did a manpower efficiency analysis for the previous days work for the managers to review in the morning. My hours were 5:30 p.m. to 3 a.m., which allowed me to continue to look for what I really wanted to do during the day.

A friend referred me to Ken Comer, a financial advisor who needed an assistant in Fort Worth. So I was his part-time assistant from 9 a.m. until 3 p.m. in Fort Worth, then off to Irving for my 5:30 p.m. job at the trucking company. Ken saw something in me I didn't see in myself and encouraged me to take a personality test that the industry heavily relied on to determine if someone had the capability to be an advisor. Reluctantly, I took the test. I remember specifically not being very careful with my answers as this really wasn't a direction I wanted to go. It was a fluke and I got a perfect score. I had promised myself that if I did well, I would try it and I had prayed that if I did get a good score, it was a sign from God that I should give it a shot.

Without Ken's insisting that I take that exam, I would not have had the wonderful career I have had the last eighteen years, and I probably wouldn't have written *Tattoo* or be writing this book. So when I say, but for the grace of God there go I, I mean it as I could easily have seen myself doing menial low-wage work because outside of having a degree, which many people had, I had no real skills to offer.

WE ALL CAN USE A BREAK

That was my break and why I believe giving someone a break is the best opportunity for any of us to have a chance at a better life as long as we rise to the challenge. You and I can be that person in someone's life, give them a chance to see something they don't see in themselves and help them reach their full potential.

Everyone deserves to buy their first home, pay off their debt, afford the family vacation, put away money for a rainy day and to one day quit working and have financial independence. If you read Ehrenreich's book, you can learn first-hand how not one of those goals is realistically achievable at the level we pay low income wage earners. What they need is hope, hope that they can do the above. One of the comments that Ehrenreich made about her co-workers from her experience in the low-wage work world was that they all for the most part worked very hard and were very proud of their work. I believe most humans when given hope, a light at the end of the tunnel, will rise to the challenge and do work worthy of the hourly wage we pay them.

I will bet that as I just reminisced about my struggle to find a career, you thought back as well to your search and you remembered the people along the way that gave you a chance, a break to help you aspire to who you are now.

OUR HOMELESS

The homeless. They are lazy, right? There is plenty of work out there if they wanted to work. Those thoughts have crossed my mind as well as possibly yours. After talking to a class called Visions, the experience opened my mind as I hope it will yours as well.

"VISIONS UNLIMITED"

In the spring of 2007, I was asked by some of the professors at Tarrant County College (TCC), Cheryl Taylor-West and Treisha Light, to help with one of their classes titled "Visions Unlimited." They wanted me to help participate in mock interviews for the students of the Visions class. It was very intriguing to me as everyone in this class of adults had one major thing in common—they were homeless.

Homeless? And they were attending classes? I have always thought it was a good idea to help put other people's lives in perspective by contemplating what life would be like "walking" in their shoes. When counseling our clients in our financial advising firm, we have learned to do this to help us have a better perspective on our client's lives to better help them.

As I considered what life must be like when you don't have your own roof over your head, I started to admire the students in this class even before I met them. I knew nothing about their situation except they didn't have the security of going to the same place every night, knowing they'd have cool air, heat or water to drink or the ability to take a hot shower. They had no home. No home and yet they went to the effort of going to class in hopes, I'm sure, of improving their current situation. Now, I have to think that if I were in their shoes, school would be the last thing on my list. I have worked 60 to 75 hours a week before when I wasn't happy with my income (even though I had a degree). So I imagine I would have just gotten three jobs at $6 or $7 dollars an hour or whatever I could find to try and improve my situation. I can't imagine that I would have thought college would have helped me.

I can't imagine studying for tests when each night I would be worrying about where to sleep and what or if I'd have something to eat. If you are one of the lucky homeless individuals who stay at a shelter, will all of your possessions be gone when you return from school or work at the end of the day? How can someone think of school or studying in an environment like that? Since I have attention

31

deficit disorder, studying was challenging enough without worrying about being able to survive. Some individuals in this class even had children, so it wasn't just their own skin they were trying to save, it was their children's lives too.

ERNEST THOMAS

I set up an interview with Dr. Ernest Thomas, TCC South president, to find out more about the Visions class that I had attended and where I experienced meeting the homeless students.

This class was designed to teach academia along with self-esteem and to allow the students to experience life on campus with the mainstream in society. It was created by an immediate need after Hurricane Katrina hit in August of 2005. Many people moved to the Dallas Fort Worth area in search of school and shelter as their lives were turned upside down after their businesses, homes and schools were destroyed. David Wells and Erma Johnson-Hadley were put in charge of an emergency response team for disaster relief at Tarrant County College. Computers were set up on the south campus of TCC to help these displaced individuals search for loved ones and register so their own whereabouts were made known. The chancellor of TCC, Dr. Leonardo De La Garza, realized many of these people were or would be, whether permanent or temporary, homeless. A homeless program that Leonardo De La Garza implemented in El Paso was used as a model to start a similar program at TCC for these individuals.

Dr. Thomas is also the individual who shared with me about the successful "Tent City" program in Seattle, Washington, which you will learn about later on in this chapter.

ERMA JOHNSON-HADLEY

When I interviewed Erma Johnson-Hadley, I already knew she was a strong, no nonsense highly-respected businesswoman, since we work closely with TCC. She also was a participant on the tour and had been appointed along with David Wells as the coordinators of the emergency response team for disaster relief at TCC which made her involved with the Visions class. I wanted to get a few comments from her. She told me that she "focused on the cause of the homeless, the mentality of the people who are there." She commented that many of the homeless she encountered were women who left their husbands with children and were unable to support themselves or their children. As long as their lives weren't in danger, she wanted to educate these women and help them prepare to leave the home, and to not leave until they were financially prepared to support themselves. Erma also states with passion that if she could—and possibly something she will do in her retirement—she would travel the country talking to woman about how to prepare themselves to be independent and thus not end up in a situation in life that causes them to be homeless.

WE CAN MAKE A DIFFERENCE

So if, as Barbara Ehrenreich discovered, one can barely survive on a $6 an hour job, then it is reasonable to think that those barely making it, unless they have another income earner in the household, are realistically close to being homeless. The wage we pay or in this case don't pay people does contribute to the homeless problem we have in this country.

WHAT WE NEED TO DO

Besides paying our employees higher wages and then challenging them to work hard to be deserving of the wage we pay them, we can learn from programs in the country already in place.

TENT CITY

Tent City is an amazingly successful program in Seattle, Washington. It is so successful that it is worthy of us taking a look at it and considering replicating it in other parts of the country.

Tent City is sponsored by the Seattle Housing and Resource Effort (SHARE) and is King County's largest shelter provider. The shelter is sponsored by private donations and costs more than $4,000 a month to support. SHARE staff is made up of formerly homeless or homeless people. Tent City has its own rules and is self-policing. To concerned citizens of Seattle, it is surprisingly well run, quiet, orderly, clean and efficiently maintained.

Tent City's location is rotated around different locations in Seattle to stay in code with city ordinances. At one of the city's roving locations, Temple Beth Ann, the executive director Sandy Voit said he hopes the group's presence will help "raise awareness" of Seattle's ongoing homeless problem.

Jeff Roderick, a resident and SHARE board member has this to say about the value of places like Tent City: "When you've got money, you don't think about those who don't. Just because we are without a house, it doesn't mean we're going to be panhandling. All we want is a safe place to get on our feet."

Of course, there are other successful programs in this country that we can learn from and implement to improve our country's homeless situation. I believe the bottom line is that when given the security of a safe place to live and hope to be able to get back on their feet, most people will do what they need to do to accomplish self-sufficiency. When given fair pay to pay their bills coupled with programs like Tent City, I believe for most of us self-sufficiency can be reached.

More self-sufficient people should result in fewer homeless people creating a less costly more efficient society for all.

It is hard for most of us to "walk in another's shoes," especially with people whose lives are so inherently different. Since you are reading this book, I'm going to take a wild guess that you are like me, and you have a roof over your head. I would like you to contemplate how easy it would be to loose everything you have, at least temporarily, like the Katrina survivors—something that you have no control over, a violent storm or fire wiping away everything that you own. It could happen to us and we'd want the opportunity to have a temporary safe haven to get back on our feet.

It is hard for us to care about issues that don't directly affect our lives. This is evident from the following remarks by Peter Davis, author of *If You Came This Way.*

THE PARADOX

Davis states, "You don't have enough money to make yourself look acceptable, so you're not accepted into a job where you could get the money to make yourself look acceptable.

"Though they are without cash for decent clothes or haircuts, not to mention dentistry, the persistently poor can be as self-conscious as the middle class about their appearance. After years without hope of changing their appearance, they become accustomed to looking poor, but they are never in doubt that they do look poor, and poorly."

HOW WE SEE "THEM"

Davis' observations, "...we dread 'them' as we walk to our cars, step over a body in the subway, hurry away from the cash machine. We build, one by one, on each other's enmity until it has become national.

"I shun them. I fear them, and, as with any enemy, I cancel them out of my thinking whenever possible."

Fort Worth Mayor Mike Moncrief knew it would be hard for most of us to even remotely imagine the life of someone homeless, and how most of us tend to look at or perceive this part of our society. So to get the business leaders in our community to care about an issue so foreign to them, he created an emotional experience that, as you will soon find from their comments, they will not soon forget.

UP CLOSE AND PERSONAL

Our forward thinking mayor Mayor Mike Moncrief wanted to improve our city's homeless situation so he took a delegation of 22 business leaders to three major cities in hopes of bringing back ideas and solutions for our city's homeless. The trip took the 22 to Los Angeles, Seattle, and Denver. Specific places visited were Skid Row in Los Angeles and the 1811 Eastlake project in Seattle.

The 22 leaders who took this three city tour were: Judi V. Bishop, YWCA of Fort Worth and Tarrant County; Vicki Jo Brozovic, City of Fort Worth; Fernando Costa, City of Fort Worth; Salvador Espino, Fort Worth City Council member; Bruce Frankel, Fort Worth Day Resource Center; Michael Guyton, Oncor Electric Delivery; Bob Herchert, Freese and Nichols; Ginny Hickman, Cook Children's Health Care System; Kathleen Hicks, Fort Worth City Council member; The Rev. Stephen Jasso, All Saints Catholic Church; Erma Johnson-Hadley, Tarrant County College District; Carol Klocek, Presbyterian Night Shelter; J.R. Labbe, Fort Worth *Star-Telegram*; Ralph McCloud, Office of Justice and Peace, Catholic Diocese of Fort Worth; Mike Moncrief, mayor of Fort Worth; Chad Morgan, Fort Worth Police Department; Rosa Navejar, Hispanic Chamber of Commerce; Don Shisler, Union Gospel Mission; Andy Taft, Downtown Fort Worth Inc.; Otis Thornton, City of Fort Worth; Glen Whitley, judge, Tarrant County Commissioners Court; and Aaron York, First Presbyterian Church, Fort Worth.

The following are quotes gathered by author J. R. Labbe with the *Star-Telegram* as she witnessed the trip first hand as a participant and interviewed attendees after the event.

FIRST STOP, SKID ROW

- "My preconceived tough love notions were turned on their head when I learned how much more humane and less expensive chronically homeless supportive housing is when compared to the cost of randomly bouncing through the health care, criminal justice and shelter systems." Andy Taft, president of Downtown Fort Worth Inc.

- "The homeless tour branded an image in my mind and heart that I will not soon forget." Mike Guyton, vice president of Oncor Electric Delivery.

- "One of the most dramatically eye-opening statements I heard during the trip was a formerly homeless woman living at the YWCA in Seattle. She said, 'It took me two months to get a job after I moved in here. I could never have gotten a job without having a home first.' She went on to explain how being unwashed, unkempt and smelling of shelters kept her from becoming employed. She told me that she had worked since high school, but her life 'had gone downhill.' Being in a home had made it possible for her to get back on her feet, manage her mental illness and be employed. Most importantly, she had her dignity and self-respect back." Carol Klocek, director of the Presbyterian Night Shelter.

- "No one on the trip will ever be able to erase the mental images of what they saw on Skid Row. A mass of slow-motion humanity lined streets and sidewalks strewn with boxes, papers and plastic bags. It was impossible to discern what might have been trash and litter from what might have been someone's possessions." J. R. Labbe, Fort Worth *Star-Telegram*.

- "The take-away lessons included dramatic dollars-and-cents analysis of the costs of leaving people homeless versus getting them into supportive housing. A Seattle study of the 75 most visible street alcoholics, those classified as public inebriates, revealed that they were costing the city and county anywhere from $40,000 to $60,000 per person annually—from $3 million to $4.5 million altogether—in emergency room, police, jail, and drunk tank use. The cost of the deteriorating good will in the business and tourism community, which grew weary of being harassed by these chronically drunken men was incalculable." J. R. Labbe.

- "The specifics as to what Fort Worth's 10-year plan for ending homelessness looks like are still in the nascent stages. But the connections among community leaders needed to develop those plans were birthed during three days of bus and plane rides, and those links are growing into mature, mutually respectful relationships." J.R. Labbe.

OTIS THORNTON

Because I live in Fort Worth, Texas, and because I had heard that our mayor, Mike Moncrief, was passionate about helping the homeless problem in our city, I decided to interview the individual our city appointed as our Homelessness Coordinator.

Our city appointed Otis Thornton as our city's homelessness coordinator in May of 2006. It is evident from my interviews with city leaders on this subject that in a very short time, he has gained heartfelt respect across the board.

His enthusiasm and passion for helping solve the chronic homeless problem in Tarrant County was captivating. At the end of our interview I had no doubts as to why our city chose him for the position and no doubts that with his guidance our city's homeless will wear a different face in the future.

A full report with all the numbers can be seen on our city's website wwwfortworthgov.org/homelessness. I want to share a few of the pertinent statistics.

What our numbers reveal from JPS (John Peter Smith hospital) emergency room:

- In 2006, the ten most expensive homeless ER users cost taxpayers more than $443,000
- Additionally, the homeless, from JPS statistics, cost taxpayers $19 million in the last three years with an average annual increase in cost in excess of $1.1 million
- 20 percent of the population of Tarrant County uses 80 percent of our resources
- MedStar (Fort Worth's ambulance service) and the Fort Worth Fire Department responded to 3,128 calls to 911 in 2006 to our four homeless shelters

A very interesting fact that came out of our interview was the comment that Otis made about the lack of accountability of the homeless. He commented, "Homelessness has lots of causes: bad choices, bad luck and bad circumstances—or, more typically, a combination of things that spiral out of control. Accountability is key; however, it must be tailored to the individual circumstance and capacities of the individual. For the chronically homeless, research suggests that providing housing and stability up front increases the likelihood that, over time, traditional and more mainstream sorts of accountability—such as exist in the structured world of work and social relationships—can be assumed by people transitioning off of the streets."

Apparently, providing shelter and a safe place to live can help to better motivate some of the formerly homeless to want to create a better life for themselves.

If we remove the chaos of their lives with permanent housing so they can deal with their issues, i.e. mental illness, addiction or just life in general, they can rise up and take care of themselves. If we provide job training and show them that there is a link between accountability and opportunity, they can transition out of homelessness.

It is evident from the 1811 Eastlake project in Seattle, referenced earlier by Labbe, that the concept of providing housing first to stop the cycle of homelessness is paramount to improving the homeless situation. Securing the basic need of shelter then motivates most individuals to start making better choices for themselves. This was brought to my attention by Kent Olson, a new team leader for Habitat for Humanity, who told me that since 1989 Habitat has built 308 homes with only eight of those homes being foreclosed. That is only a three percent failure rate, which is pretty good odds in my book. In case you don't know about Habitat for Humanity, to qualify for a free home that is built for them, the individual cannot own a home, they must put in 300 hours of work on the home (they feel ownership I'm sure), and lastly, they must be within 30 to 70 percent of the median income for a family of four. When given the chance for a start by having a safe home/shelter to stay in, people step up to the challenge, and 97 percent of them responsibly pay their mortgage so they can keep it. So when you hear "housing first" I hope you will remember the 1811 Eastlake project and the stats I shared about Habitat.

At the end of our interview, I asked Otis about the source of his obvious passion for the homeless. He told me, "When you have seen what I have seen, it's not hard." Otis mentioned that he has seen first-hand over 6,300 homeless people in the course of one year.

A census of our homeless is required by Housing and Urban Development (HUD) each January, often our coldest month. So prior to the three-city tour that Mayor Moncrief organized, he had Otis brief the participants of the tour on Tarrant County's homeless. A tour of the largest section of town where our homeless congregate was also part of the preparation for the trip.

YOUR OWN CITY

As you contemplate this one area where we can all give back to humanity and what we can be doing in all of our cities to help our homeless go from despair to self-sufficiency, I'd like to leave you with two more quotes from Peter Davis' book.

"Most of us do not think of the underclass as men and women like ourselves, with children like our own, with needs and wants fully comparable to those we satisfy daily.

"With a national will that begins with national consciousness, we can do the underclass the favor, both before and beyond policy or program, of considering them human."

MARKETING VIA THE HUMAN FACTOR

Accept the fact that you will need to change to create better employee relations, better customer service, and better partners or alliances. Additionally, if your company chooses to give back to humanity, then you will become known for The Human Factor and your reputation will precede you in business. By paying fair wages, we will in turn ease our social benefit programs and help our homeless instead of adding to their burden. Your customers will want to do business with you because you value The Human Factor. Because you show you care, you will motivate and even empower your customers to care. In turn, they will contagiously spread the word about your business, marketing it for you.

THE TEN ATTRIBUTES
OF THE HUMAN FACTOR

"An empowered organization is one in which individuals have the knowledge, skill, desire and opportunity to personally succeed in a way that leads to collective organizational success."

—Stephen R. Covey
Author and motivational speaker

"Never doubt the fact that a group of thoughtful, committed citizens can change the world; indeed, it's the only thing that ever does."

—Margaret Mead (1901-1987)
Well-known anthropologist
and best selling author of *Coming of Age in Samoa*

As consumers, we need to choose companies that we do business with or work for that value the attributes of The Human Factor. As business owners, we need to create companies that value The Human Factor.

Here are the ten attributes that will help you create a business worth talking about. These attributes will also help you as you contemplate where to spend your hard-earned money. These attributes will also help you create a business worth telling a story about. That story will become what causes your customers to market for you as they spread the story of your business to others creating your marketing virus.

THE TEN ATTRIBUTES

1. Invest in the Best Technology
2. Hire the Right People
3. Hire Diversity to Market Globally
4. Listen to Your Employees
5. Hold Employees Accountable
6. Think of Your Employees as Customers
7. Provide a Good Environment for Your Employees to Grow
8. Listen to Your Customer
9. Give Back to Humanity and Encourage Employees to do the Same
10. Create a Story

1. <u>INVEST IN THE BEST TECHNOLOGY</u>

By all means, invest in the best technology you can manage and use it to learn more about your customers; get to know them on a human level, their likes, dislikes, their buying habits. No one knows this fact better than the hotel industry.

In an interview with Mark Hamilton, president of the Hospitality Information and Technology Association (HITA), I was reminded of the fact that hotels have used technology to know their customers for the last several years.

Customization

Mark shared with me the philosophy of The Wyndham Hotels, which are owned by Cendant Corporation. Wyndham has a program called Wyndham by request. This technology is centralized so Wyndham can keep track of its customers' preferences and history. A profile is kept for each customer by logging all visits to Wyndham. Data that is tracked are customer's favorite music, television stations, and newspaper preference. As the customer visits Wyndham, he or she achieves different levels based on the number of stays resulting in free services like phone and internet access in the customer's room. Once Wyndham guests hit specific levels, guests can fill out a survey letting the hotel know what paper they prefer so that specific paper is in front of their door in the morning. Also, guests can be reminded of their favorite television shows and the channel and time they are on in whatever part of the country the guests happen to be staying.

We as consumers are smart enough to know why the television screen reminds us of our favorite shows and our preferred paper is in front of our door, which could be different than our hotel neighbor. This is a form of marketing and customer service. Even though we gave the hotel this information and we know it is all done by a computer, let me ask you, when this happens do you or I walk away feeling any less special? When I turn on the television, the screen may read, "Welcome to Wyndham, Ms. Turner, your favorite show *Law and Order* is on channel 15 in our area and airs at 10 p.m." This experience can be replicated all over the country from New York to San Francisco and everywhere in between.

Invest in the best technology and then use that technology to get to know your customers, and their human interests. You will make them feel special and create a story to be told of their experience with you.

Make Them Feel Special

Authors and consultants Donald Peppers and Martha Rodgers describe a "One-to-One" world in which companies grow not by selling their goods to a larger audience, but by learning how to sell more products and services to existing customers. They go on to state that, "This simple turn of business thinking is predicted by companies increasing ability to compile sophisticated information on what their customer needs and then respond nimbly to this data."

In *Douglas McGregor Revisited*, the authors state, "Yet computers, which can customize products, cannot humanize them. For that you need humans. With every transaction, people become more important in the process. That's because the ability to customize a product to the individual makes the relationship with the customer the key transaction. Again, the human relationship serves as the platform upon which these companies deliver greater value."

Mark Hamilton's experience is in the technology side of the hotel industry. He worked for Radiant Systems, which bought the software developed by Aloha's Brian Cook. Brian Cook started Aloha in his garage in Bedford, Texas. Several years ago he sold his company to the large conglomerate Radiant Systems. Aloha's software capabilities allowed it to record in detail consumer's preferences and then stored these records for future use. Mark commented on the sales force of Aloha and Radiant Systems and how they had to rely on the reputation and relationship they had with the customer. We are talking about technology, but we still need human insight to be successful in distributing it. Mark continued, "Products all look the same on paper. So when it comes down to it, the bottom line is do we have a strong enough relationship with that customer so they believe the product will do what the sales representative says it will do? And the customer has confidence in that fact because of the strength of our relationship."

2. <u>HIRE THE RIGHT EMPLOYEES</u>

I had the opportunity to interview Randy Eisenman, founder of Handango, Inc. I asked him what he needed to do to remain competitive globally in his industry, which is the technology of hand-held devices. His answer was, "Hire the right people." He went on to say the second way to remain competitive is to develop deep relationships with customers. "It starts with the people," Randy summarized. "We listen to what our partners, employees, and customers tell us and then deliver what is important to them. The more information you can gather from people the better the perspective you have to make decisions, which allows the company to make better decisions."

An interesting fact that came out in the interview was that Handango had expanded into Europe, and that they had just hired someone to manage the European office. I asked Randy why go to the expense of an overseas office? With technology today, couldn't they just work with their European markets from their United States base? He told me that when doing business in Europe, the Europeans wanted you to have a physical presence. Vodafone, the leading international mobile communications group in the world, valued face-to-face meetings and if Handango wanted to be a player there, they had to physically set up shop, another testament to the value of "The Human Factor."

3. **HIRE DIVERSITY TO COMPETE GLOBALLY**

As our world continues to rapidly globalize, we will need a diverse work force to compete on a global basis. In the "I Have a Vision" chapter later in this book is an example of how companies hire diversity to compete and market globally.

4. **LISTEN TO YOUR EMPLOYEES**

Linda Kaplan of the Kaplan Thaler Group, has a "fireside chat" once a month with her employees. "People can simply talk to me about what's on their mind." Kaplan does this to hear what employees are thinking or fearing, and to let them know they are important and "heard" in her organization.

In *Tattoo*, I discussed the Gallup Organization which coined the phrase "employee engagement." Gallup uses a 12-question test called the Q 12 to determine how engaged employees are in their company. When you and I engage our employees, they feel their opinions count and state that their development is encouraged and they receive praise for their efforts.

I'm sure you aren't much different than us and our firm, when it comes to your staff's salaries and benefits. Your costs are rising and you probably think the only way to keep great employees is by increasing their salary and benefits. But a study done in 2000 by the University of Dallas found that there was no correlation between CEO pay and engagement, or even CEO pay and company loyalty. Three of Gallup's 12 questions are key to creating "engaged" employees: first, the mission/purpose of my company makes me feel my job is important; second, at work, my opinions seem to count; and third, this last year, I have had opportunities to learn and grow.

The only way we can get our employees' opinions, find out if they are learning and growing, and determine if the mission or purpose of the company creates the feeling of importance to our employees is by listening to them.

5. <u>HOLD EMPLOYEES ACCOUNTABLE</u>

I interviewed Julie Miller and Brian Bedford, of Miller Bedford, an organizational consulting firm out of Austin, Texas. I asked them, "What is the number one reason you see teams you train or companies you work with fail?" Their answer was companies or teams not holding their employees accountable. Julie and Brian spend hours consulting with teams and coming up with solutions to help client's companies be more successful, only to see them fail for this one reason. Even though these companies agree that the solutions make sense and that change is needed to be more successful, management won't make employees accountable so the plan fails. The goal setting and planning that the team does is not followed through on and unfortunately these companies not only wasted their time and money going through this process, they never saw the benefit that could have resulted from implementing the needed changes.

One of the key benefits the Miller Bedford consulting team gives to companies is listening to employees for the company. Employees are encouraged to talk openly and honestly about issues or roadblocks, and what is going right and what is going wrong from the employee perspective.

Both Brian and Julie had backgrounds in technology so today they spend their time consulting to high technology businesses. I would imagine especially in high technology companies, it would be easy for companies to loose sight of the human side of business. This is where a team like Miller Bedford can really bring value.

On a Human Factor note, The Miller Bedford group also gives back to the community as well. They are involved in the local food pantry, they do charity work through their Presbyterian church and do pro bono work for The United Way as a way to donate their time for a cause.

6. <u>THINK OF YOUR EMPLOYEE AS A CUSTOMER</u>

In interviews and from my research and reading, one of the conclusions for success seems to be hiring the right people. If hiring the right people is vitally important to building a successful organization, then doesn't it make sense to treat them well, as you would your best customer? You don't want to lose your best customer and you don't want to lose and replace your best employees either.

This concept will be discussed in more detail in the chapter "I Have a Vision."

7. <u>PROVIDE A GOOD ENVIRONMENT</u>
<u>FOR YOUR EMPLOYEES TO GROW</u>

Mihaly Csikszentmihalyi, author of the best-selling book *Flow: The Psychology of Optimal Experience,* writes that attention, creating an environment in which there is never a moment to waste, allows employees to stand ready to take on whatever challenges they may face dealing with customers throughout the day. "Because it is also required to make any other mental events—such as remembering, thinking, feeling, and making decisions—happen there, it is useful to think of it as psychic energy. Attention is like energy in that without it, no work can be done."

In Edward E. Lawler III's book *Treat People Right!,* he states, "Organizations must develop ways to treat their employees so that they are motivated and satisfied; employees must behave in ways that help their organizations become effective and high-performing. Today's organizations must focus on their people."

Remember one of Gallup's questions for the Q 12 to create employee "engagement?" "This past year I have had the opportunity to grow."

Encourage Creativity

In Creativity in Business by M. Ray and R. Myers, Ray, who is the creator of Stanford Business School courses on creativity, has three assumptions: (1) that creativity is essential for health, happiness, and success in all areas of life, including business; (2) that "creativity is within everyone;" and (3) that even though it is within everyone, it is "covered over by the Voice of Judgment."

Ray's creativity class stems partly from Howard Gardner's Project Zero at Harvard that created intelligence tests for babies. The project found that up to age four, almost all children were at the genius level in many traits and characteristics including spatial, kinesthetic, musical, interpersonal, mathematical, and linguistic. By age twenty, the percentage of children at genius level was down to only ten percent, and over age twenty, the genius level of the subjects sank to two percent.

Ray states that everyone asks, where did it go? "It didn't go anywhere; it's covered up by the Voice of Judgment," states Ray. "What we're trying to do is set up situations where people can attack the Voice of Judgment and access their deeper creativity."

That is really an incredible statistic and speaks to the fact that we all have within us more potential than we realize; we just don't believe in ourselves enough to achieve it. *The Power of Positive Thinking* by Norman Vincent Peale and *The Power of Intention* by Robert W.

Dyer are books that confirm this as well. And I believe sometimes it takes someone else to see what we are capable of before we can see it in ourselves. If we can instill that confidence and hope, it can mean the difference in becoming like the people in Barbara Ehrenreich's book who were frustrated and barely getting by to people who reach their potential and have the ability to live out their dreams.

8. <u>LISTEN TO YOUR CUSTOMER</u>

Larry Wilson, author of, *Stop Selling Start Partnering,* states that his entire book is "...about thinking differently about customers and, as a result, creating new and more powerful relationships with your best clients."

You and I know the world has become more and more competitive. Your competition today is coming from inside and outside of United States borders. Wilson goes on to say, "The bottom line in the eyes of your customers is there is not much difference between what you offer and what your competitor offers."

9. <u>GIVE BACK TO HUMANITY</u> <u>AND ENCOURAGE EMPLOYEES TO DO THE SAME</u>

Joe Marconi in his book, *Cause Marketing,* defines cause marketing as "...the means through which a company, a nonprofit organization, or a similar entity markets an image, product, service, or message for mutual benefits."

Business for Social Responsibility (BSR), founded in 1992, is a membership organization for companies seeking to sustain their commercial success in ways that demonstrate respect for ethical values, people, communities and the environment.

According to Marconi, North American companies spent an estimated 630 million dollars on sponsorships related to cause marketing in 1999, an increase of almost 500 percent over the reported 1990 spending. Figures since then have risen substantially.

In the early 1990's "...companies were learning that their images and the public's perception of them did indeed matter. Good corporate citizenship was rewarded with consumer loyalty and good word-of-mouth, a term implying community approval."

In his 1999 book *The Art of Cause Marketing,* Richard Earle states, "Six in ten Americans say they'd buy first from a company that backs a cause they support."

The Business in the Community's 1998 corporate research study conducted by Research International (UK), Ltd. did two key research studies: one was a consumer study in 1996; the other was a corporate research study done in 1998. Here is what was concluded from their research:

1996 Consumer Study

- Eighty-six percent of consumers are more likely to buy a product associated with a cause or issue.
- Eighty-six percent of consumers have a more positive image of a company they believe is doing something to make the world a better place.
- Sixty-four percent of consumers feel companies should make cause-related marketing a part of their standard business practice.

1998 Corporate Research Study

- More than 70 percent of chief executives, marketing directors, and community affairs directors believe that cause-related marketing will grow in importance to their organizations in the coming years.
- Seventy-five percent feel cause-related marketing can enhance corporate or brand reputations.
- Eighty-one percent of marketing directors believe that companies should address the social issues of the day.

- Fifty-eight percent of marketing directors agree that cause-related marketing strategy provides companies with the opportunity to address business objectives and social issues at the same time.

If doing the right thing, making our world a better place to live, and just feeling better about what you create isn't enough to encourage you to consider giving back to humanity and encouraging your employees to do the same, then maybe those statistics will motivate you.

The book *Cause Marketing* references a number of companies who have received awards and have been recognized because of their contribution to society. A list of these companies is included for your information on page 180.

10. <u>CREATE A STORY</u>

Create a story to be told by your customer because you value The Human Factor. That is what you become known for: how you treat people, your employees, your customers, and humanity. That becomes your unique marketing message, a passionate story behind your business that causes people to talk and spread your message.

Chip and Dan Heath's book, *Made to Stick, Why Some Ideas Survive and Others Die,* notes, "The story's power, then, is twofold: It provides simulation (knowledge about how to act) and inspiration (motivation to act). Note that both benefits, simulation and inspiration, are geared to generating action. A credible idea makes people believe. An *emotional* idea makes people care. And... the right stories make people act."

In the book *Presence, An Exploration of Profound Change in People, Organizations and Society*, the group of authors discuss how over the last two hundred years, technology has created change in how humans relate to each other in the workplace that "...create growing technological power and diminishing human development and wisdom." The authors go on to state, "This means growing in our sense of connection with nature and with one another and learning to live in ways that naturally cultivate our capacity to be human." The authors state further that to be successful in organizations today, "We will need to use the heart more, which means the quality of our being and relationships with one another become more and more central in allowing an organization to flourish."

Why Now

Why is The Human Factor more important now than ever?

According to the authors of *Douglas McGregor, Revisited Managing the Human Enterprise*, "Our age of technological dazzle has led to a paradox. And as such, companies are finding that their enduring source of competitive advantage rests within their human capital. "Those businesses that thrive today are not necessarily those with the most valuable resources, the greatest market share, or the most capital (though none of those hurt). Rather, those businesses that are able to tap their human potential in the most productive manner are the ones who enjoy success."

McGregor, one of the forefathers of management theory and one of the top five business thinkers of all time according to the authors of *Douglas McGregor, Revisited,* "...proved that to truly succeed, companies must cultivate an organization that is built on enduring relationships with the workforce and customers."

On Ed Horrell's talk show "Talk About Service," Ed states, "Service levels are discussed constantly, and yet what fascinates me is that so many companies continue to be oblivious to what their customers are thinking and saying about their service!" To do research for his book, *The Kindness Revolution,* Horrell went out to find the best companies who delivered the best in customer service. He found, "...I am convinced of the fact that values play the most significant role in determining how customers and employees are treated in any organization. Notice, I didn't say 'a' significant role. I said, 'the' significant role."

To create value in an organization you need humans.

With these attributes you will become known for valuing The Human Factor and create a story that will be told about your organization that will become your unique differentiating factor. This unique factor will become your best marketing tool.

Get Them to Care

Because we are all moving so fast today and are so inundated with advertising, most of which we ignore, we need our customers to "care" about wanting others to do business with us. And just as Mayor Moncrief knew that he had to get our business leaders to care about our homeless and so created an emotional experience for them, we create an environment where our customers care. They care so much about what we have created because of what we stand for, that they want everyone in their world to do business with us, too. These ten Human Factor attributes create this environment resulting in customer zealots who can't help but go out and market our businesses for us.

YOU GET WHAT YOU PAY FOR

"It's a very sobering feeling to be up in space and realize that one's safety factor was determined by the lowest bidder on a government contract."

—Alan B. Shepard Jr.

First U.S. astronaut in space, 1961

"Sometimes the best way to change the world is by getting the big players to do the right things for the wrong reasons, because waiting for them to do the right things for the right reasons can mean waiting forever."

—Thomas L. Friedman,

The World is Flat

When our parents, told us this phrase "you get what you pay for" as kids, they were talking about the quality or value in what we bought. If it was perceived as too inexpensive, my parents would tell me it would not last as long and it was better to spend more money and get a better quality product that would last longer.

That is not what I am talking about here. By now, you can probably tell that one of my missions in life is to get people to think differently about a word—like Virus—or an idea or a concept.

Remember, as Oliver Wendell Holmes said, "Once a mind is stretched to a new idea, it never goes back to its original dimension."

I am talking about companies that tout the lowest prices, and quite possibly they are, but the low prices we receive as a consumer, we pay for in higher property taxes because the employees of these kinds of companies don't make enough to support themselves.

So the next time you run into a discount store to get a CD, groceries, hardware, school supplies, or whatever your purchase, consider the potential cost of those low prices to our society and economy, before you spend your money there. We pay a price to get those lowest prices, but we do not think of it that way because it is hidden in the taxes we pay to support the employees of corporations who do not get paid enough to take care of themselves. As the cost of health care in our society continues to escalate, this problem is only going to get worse, and our taxes are going to continue to climb.

As I do speaking engagements across the country, I feel one of the best ways to get a point across is to ask thought provoking questions. So here you go...

I am referring to a specific company here and according to Thomas L. Friedman, author of *The World is Flat*, their "biggest competitors complain that they have had to cut health care benefits and create a lower wage tier to compete." Friedman goes on to state, this one company, "pays less and covers less than most big companies."

The following provides information on this company which you may find of interest; I know I did.

WOULD YOU DO BUSINESS
WITH A COMPANY WHO...

- The company has "pursued cost cutting and profit margins to such a degree that whatever social benefits it is offering with one hand, it is taking away with the other." Friedman

- It makes full-time employees wait six months before qualifying for health care, and part-time employees have to wait at least two years to be eligible. *New York Times*, November 1, 2004

- It requires employees to cover 33% of health care costs. *New York Times*, November 1, 2004.

- The company pays employees $8 an hour or $1,200 per month, making health care coverage unaffordable for many employees even though coverage is offered. *New York Times*, November 1, 2004.

- As a result of all of this, only 45% of their workers have health insurance. *New York Times*, November 1, 2004. And according to Friedman, 68% of their workforce is on Medicaid. Friedman also states that "...when you totally flatten your supply chain, you also take a certain element of humanity out of life."

- During an interview with Liza Featherstone, author of *Selling Women Short*, Salon.com November 22, 2004, she noted that 80% of the company's corporate campaign contributions go to Republicans, but Republicans tend not to support the types of public assistance programs that the company's employees depend on.

- In her book, Featherstone states that we are affected as taxpayers by these corporations who pay workers so little in wages that they can't support themselves. Featherstone notes, "Because they usually require incremental health insurance, public housing, food stamps... employees are not able to be self-sufficient."

- In 2005, U. S. tax dollars subsidized nearly 1.4 billion dollars (yes, that's a "b") in employee health care costs. It is estimated that over the next five years in health care costs alone this company will cost American taxpayers more than 9 billion dollars. (*Door County Compass*)

- The company caused one of its vendors to cut 1,000 jobs because it wouldn't pay the extra cost of goods that had gone up because a key material went up in price although every other vendor of this company accepted the cost hike. By the way, the cost hike was 20 cents. Would it have mattered if this chain would have sold the product for 20 cents more? I doubt it.

- It has been quoted as a cost driven, low-price, low road towards U.S. competitiveness versus an innovation-oriented high road to U.S. competitiveness, like Starbucks.

- The Nathan Cummings Foundation which takes issue with the free market, has this to say on its website: "The technological, economic, globalization and communications revolutions are causing transformations that create challenges to social and economic justice and the ability to foster equitable and sustainable economic growth that promotes individual opportunity, social well-being and community."

Friedman also states that "...when you totally flatten your supply chain, you also take a certain element of humanity out of life."

DEAD HORSE

Forgive me if you feel this horse is dead, but I have a few more.

- The company sued a local community for blocking its plan to put a store on a road which caused the town's citizens' taxes to go up to pay legal fees the suit generated. Here's an even scarier thought: if that city council wasn't carrying liability insurance for its board members, it could have caused personal bankruptcy for its city council members. I tried and find out if this actually ever happened somewhere and couldn't find it. I hope there isn't a case out there like that, but it very well could happen.

- On the above case, one of the city council members commented, "What is the point of having a city council, if a company can come in and say "the heck with you. We're doing what we want to anyway?" Exactly!

- In one metropolitan city in Central America, this company caused thirty supermarkets to close after this store saturated the area. A store opening in another city quickly put out of business: four clothing stores, four grocery stores, a stationary store, a fabric store, and a lawn-and-garden center (and a partridge in a pear tree, sorry couldn't resist that). The local paper there is now struggling as it lost major ad revenues from these closures.

If this chain as well as other "chains" that keep cutting costs of products, benefits and wages to employees destroys the economic fabric of our country and entrepreneurial spirit, ask yourself what kind of a world will we live in? That entrepreneurial spirit is one element that makes this country such a great place in which to live.

Here's the question: Once they drive out all of the other businesses in our communities, what will stop them once they have no competition (virtually a monopoly), from raising their prices?

I'm going to let that sink in for a minute.

OUR LIVES AS CONSUMERS

I believe we do have a social responsibility to help our brothers and sisters here and around the world. What better way than by choosing to do business with companies who value The Human Factor? After all, you and I will always be consumers, won't we? We will heat and cool our homes (even if in the future that energy source comes from something different than what we use now), we will eat food, buy and drive cars, and have clothes to wear.

ON A SIDE NOTE

When people become concerned about the stock market because of its volatility, discussing the fact that we will always be consumers is often something we share with clients when we counsel them, to help put in perspective what those money managers are buying. The price of goods and services has always gone up over time. Professional money managers buy stock in the companies that we buy from as consumers, so we will always benefit from that growth through our equity holdings. You will never wake up and not be a consumer, right? So we as consumers help drive the prices of the goods of the companies that the professional money managers buy, right? And the cost of those goods will always increase over time, on average 3 percent a year, according to consulting firm Ibbotson Associates®.

TO PUT THINGS IN PERSPECTIVE

It is always amazing to me that when you project those numbers out into the future, they can be quite daunting. As an example, if I want, say $10,000 a month in retirement, in twenty years, that monthly number inflated at 3 percent per year is $18,061 in the year 2027 when I am 64. What is also amazing to me is that some people we counsel want to refrain from using equities in their portfolio, because they go up and down and a certificate of deposit or money market does not. But that certificate of deposit or money market may earn the investor 3 percent before taxes. So 3 percent before taxes equates to something less than that after taxes are taken into account. I am already behind and have no room for growth to give myself that needed raise every few years to keep up with the cost of living. That is like putting your money under your mattress for twenty years. As long as your house doesn't burn down, you can take it out at retirement, but it will only be a third of the goods and services of twenty years prior because of inflation.

I am a very simple person, and feel that my knowledge has grown from the people I have had the opportunity to meet and the books I have read. I have had the fortunate opportunity to study over the last three years under two professors, Dr. Sam Thomas, Professor of Finance at the Weatherford School of Management, Case Western Reserve University, and Dr. Harold Longolis, a Harvard professor and president and founder of a financial consulting group specializing in behavioral education. Dr. Thomas is a mathematician and statistician who tests what we use to develop and customize our clients' portfolios, modern portfolio theory. (By the way, we have had clients ask us if this theory stills works, then why didn't my previous advisor or all advisors for that matter use it? I honestly don't know why, except to say ignorance, laziness, apathy {or maybe they just don't care enough}). If this applies to you, I would personally suggest your asking your advisor why he or she doesn't use the theory and if you don't like the answer, find someone who does use this proven strategy, called modern portfolio theory.

80 PERCENT OF CONSUMERS

Interestingly, while at The Wharton School of the University of Pennsylvania this year, we were told that a study done by the university revealed that 80 percent of consumers within two years of retirement will fire their financial advisor. That is amazing. And I believe there are two reasons as to why. One, the idea of us needing our retirement monies to last 20, 30, or even 40 years is very daunting. The other idea about this is that if these people had been taken care of over the last several years by a qualified advisor, they wouldn't be firing them, which gets back to my earlier statement that many advisors don't really care, are lazy or apathetic, which we can tell when we analyze clients' portfolios.

Sorry for getting on my soapbox for a minute, but it is a pet peeve of mine and a real disservice to the investors in this country and our reputation as advisors. "The best competition is good competition," from my first book *Tattoo*, because when we meet someone who has had a bad experience with an advisor, we start off the relationship with them being skeptical of us that we really are better and different than their previous advisor, which makes earning their trust harder and harder.

Now most of us need someone to make us accountable for doing the right thing when it comes to our own money. That is where Harold Longolis comes in. He was our psychology professor while attending the financial planning institute at Harvard. He basically told us that what Sam shared with us is great, but most people without an advisor will make the wrong decisions at the wrong time. Therefore, people need advisors to help them do what is good for them when it comes to their money—even when they don't want or feel like doing what is good for them. Years like 2002, when we had a very volatile market and one of the worst markets in U.S. history, could really show you how good your advisor is.

THE VALUE OF WORKING WITH PROFESSIONALS

As an example of the value in hiring professionals, we know several pilots who work for Fort Worth based American Airlines. I frequently hear people complain about how much pilots get paid for only working a few weeks a month. Now sometimes I can get a little defensive when I feel people are being critical and a little unfair to those they criticize. On the worst flight I have ever been on coming back from Boston one year in a terrible storm, the ride was extremely bumpy and you could see a tornado circling over the Dallas Fort Worth airport. The tension on the plane was obvious as everyone became ghostly quiet. I felt like standing up and saying, "How much do you think this pilot is worth right now?" Fearing for your life can bring an amazing perspective. So like those pilots, the real rocky years in the financial markets are where the truly great advisors shine.

BACK TO...

You get what you pay for. So back to the main idea for this chapter. We have a responsibility as consumers and concerned citizens to consider with whom we do business. Do the companies we patronize treat their employees fairly via pay and benefits, so that these companies contribute positively to our society? Or do they contribute negatively to our society and actually add to the burden of our already strained social benefit systems?

Because remember, the next time you walk through a store and consider where you will spend your hard-earned money, we as a society do get what we pay for.

HALLOWEEN, RED DYE NO. 2, AND O.J. SIMPSON

These three very different things—Halloween, red dye #2 and O.J. Simpson—actually have a lot in common as you will soon understand. Their similarity has to do with the power we have as consumers and how we can vote with our voice, our pocketbooks, and our actions. Remember in the early 1970s when Halloween became a holiday to truly be feared for one apparent reason: the belief all across the country that someone, somewhere, somehow was putting razor blades in our children's apples?

Now, I would have been about ten then and I never received an apple or a piece of fruit for that matter, while I was out trick or treating. However, I do remember my parents sitting my brother and sister and me down before we headed out to trick or treat telling us that if we did receive a piece of fruit, we would throw it away as opposed to worrying about if my parents could cut it up enough to avoid the allusive razor blade that would possibly be lurking inside the host fruit.

Our local hospital offered to x-ray our fruit for free, but was it really worth all that effort, when we really just wanted the candy anyway? If the razor blade story made it to a little town of 3,000 people in the middle of nowhere in Kansas, it could make it anywhere, right? And probably did.

RAZOR BLADES IN APPLES

So where did the story cr rumor about razor blades in apples come from? Sociologists Joel Best and Gerald Horiuchi studied every reported Halloween incident since 1958. They went back to see if there had been any recorded deaths of children on Halloween due to the sabotage of Halloween candy or apples.

READ AND BE AMAZED...

They did in fact find two recorded deaths on Halloween and they did involve the tainting of Halloween candy.

The first case was a five-year-old child in California who discovered his uncle's heroin stash and subsequently overdosed. It happened around Halloween, and to cover up the heroin the family didn't want anyone to know they had, the parents sprinkled the child's Halloween candy with heroin.

The other account is equally if not more horrifying. A father tainted his son's candy with cyanide hopefully to collect on the insurance policy the father had on the infant.

Based on these two stories, it's not our neighbors we should be concerned about, is it? It's the parents!

Now of course we have to be cautious and watchful of our children so we don't put them at undue risk. There are people in this world who we can't trust with our children, but by being sensible we can allow our children to enjoy this fun tradition and have a good reason to chat with our neighbors.

Is it not as amazing to you as it was to me that the razor blade story spread like wildfire across the country and caused most of us to forever alter a Halloween tradition meant to be fun? To this day hospitals offer to x-ray children's candy and public service announcements warn to not trick or treat in neighborhoods but to go to the local community center or school where candy can be distributed on a somewhat controlled and supervised basis. It seems a shame since there are no apparent factual incidents to substantiate this fear—just stories people have recounted and retold for thirty plus years.

FRONT PORCHES

Without a doubt, the whole "razor blades in apples" phenomenon is an example of why we have become mistrusting of our neighbors and often first think the "worst" in others instead of the "best." We pull in our driveways, close the garage door, and are in for the night never to return until it is time to go to work the next day. We don't mingle out front and get to know our neighbors and neighborhoods. This is partly because of our busy schedules but also because of mistrusts developed in our society.

I am as guilty of this as anyone, but I want to share a story about how I met a really cool neighbor and how a friendship formed because of one thing... a front porch. I have lived on the same street in Fort Worth at three different locations. This may seem odd but I love my little neighborhood and just kept moving into a nicer home to rent until I found one on the same street to buy. I ran almost every day down my street with my two dogs. There was a certain neighbor who would normally be hanging out on his big front porch always standing and reading the newspaper and smoking a cigarette. I would wave from across the street and he would wave back. This literally went on for ten years. I never saw him anywhere else but he knew me as "the lady who ran the two dogs" and I knew him as "the man reading the newspaper, smoking on his front porch." Then one day I saw him in the grocery store and he said, "Hey, you are the lady with the two dogs," and of course you know what I said back to him. For the first time we introduced ourselves.

WE SHARED A COMMON DREAM

The very next time I went running, I made it a point to run across the street and stop and talk to him. We shared with each other that we had always dreamed of owning a Harley-Davidson motorcycle. We continued this casual friendship over the next few years and chatted, he on his porch and me with my dogs. About two years later, I took the motorcycle safety class and soon thereafter I bought my first Harley. I hadn't seen my neighbor Rod to tell him and it happened rather quickly. Ironically the very next weekend, I heard a familiar rumble in my driveway. I told myself Rod had bought a bike. I went outside and there he was with his new Fat Boy Harley and a big grin on his face. We couldn't believe that we both had bought them within a week of each other and had never discussed doing so or when we were planning to do it. For the next several years, we rode our bikes all over Fort Worth and the surrounding areas virtually every weekend, at least once. We also took a trip to Austin to the annual bike rally there. His wife Ann went with us and we had a great time.

He unfortunately has passed away, but I am very thankful for his friendship and I now share a close friendship with Ann and her new husband Gene. With the suspicion we often have of our neighbors, it is unlikely that I would have ever met Rod had it not been for his front porch.

Years ago I had been to a neighborhood meeting where there was a discussion about front porches and how all new homes were required to have them. Studies showed a reduction in crime because people spend time on their porches. They see what goes on in their neighborhood, get to know their neighbors, and as a result make their neighborhood a safer place to live.

Needless to say, I'm thankful for front porches not just for a safer neighborhood but for helping me meet one of my dearest friends.

BACK TO RAZOR BLADES

It is amazing to think that to get this message of fear to spread like a virus across the country, no advertising dollars were spent. Corporations spend millions of dollars on ads that often can't get our attention.

Instead of advertising, all we need is a good story, the more emotional, the more compelling and heart touching, the better. That coupled with a great customer base to spread the story, and the only thing that will be scared is our competition.

A BRIEF HISTORY OF M&M'S®

When M&M's candies were first introduced in 1940 they were an immediate hit. The candies were named after the founders, Forest Mars and Bruce Murrie. Their first big customer was the United States Army, which preferred the sugar-coated candies for the troops because they "melted in the mouth, not in the hand." The candy continues to be a popular selection among consumers. Mars, Incorporated Family of Companies, the company that makes M&M's, has done some unique marketing by getting the consumer involved in actually voting on their favorite colors. This is truly a company that listens to what its customers want and then makes changes based on the feedback the customer gives them.

Originally there were six colors—red, orange, yellow, green, brown and violet. In 1949, tan replaced violet. In 1993, a reported ten million customers voted on what their favorite existing colors were, and what would be a good color to add. Voila ... we now no longer have tan M&M's but blue instead. This made customers feel they were a part of the organization by allowing them to vote on what they wanted, participate, and see the results of their actions.

Now you can buy online custom-made M&M's and have them imprinted with your own message of two lines with up to eight characters in seventeen different colors. So you can say, "Marry me," "I love you"—get as creative as you want! Of course, you can get them packaged in bright colorful boxes and neat gift packages and have them shipped directly to that special person's door. My book *Tattoo* discusses customization and how we can get customers to want to do business with us if we customize products or services to make them feel special.

Mars is definitely a company that listens to its customer and then delivers what they want. I have to think that is one reason for the company's continued success—besides the taste of course, especially if you do like I do and put them in the freezer! Yum!

RED M&M'S VANISH

In 1976, Mars discontinued red M&M's for one main reason, the consumer. In 1976, the United States Food and Drug Administration delisted one particular red food coloring, FD&C No. 2 (amaranth), also known as Red Dye No. 2. The public believed that Red Dye No. 2 was now a serious health threat and so balked at buying M&M's altogether. Their rationale apparently was that there are red M&M's, and so Red Dye No. 2 must have been used in making them, so don't buy M&M's.

It didn't matter that Red Dye No. 2 was never used by Mars to make M&M's. To get consumers to start buying the candies again, the company simply removed the red ones from production.

There are two interesting points here. Mars continued to make red ones because in the international markets, the consumers weren't concerned about the red color and so were continuing to buy them.

The other point is that Mars also makes Skittles® candies. Have you ever looked at a pack of original Skittles? You guessed it. In the original packages, many of them were red. But for some reason the consumer didn't balk at buying them so Mars continued to make red Skittles at the same time they were deleting red M&M's! What we do as consumers doesn't have to make sense, does it? The old saying of "perception is everything" truly applies here.

RED M&M'S COME BACK

So how did we get red M&M's back? The consumer of course! Apparently, the red ones were missed and upon repeated persistent requests by numerous consumers in 1987, red M&M's were reintroduced in the United States market.

This is another testament to the power we have as consumers to demand what we want from companies. If they don't comply, if there are enough of us, we can invoke change.

FEBRUARY 2007

On February 27, 2007, we woke up in the United States and discovered the Chinese stock market was not feeling so well the night before and had a significant drop in its value. The Dow Jones Industrials Average reacted and dropped a total of roughly 400 points that day. At the same time, the media had been feeding us stories about how many United States businesses were profiting and growing due to the tremendous growth that was happening in the Chinese economy.

So when we heard of a drop in the Chinese economy, we reacted, panicked a bit, and started the day selling shares on the New York Stock Exchange.

Later that day on the NYSE, a computer glitch caused the monitors to not record the gradual drop that was occurring in the market. The drop was actually taking place over an hour and a half, and it was about a 200 point drop, which would be alarming. When the computers caught up with where the market was, it had dropped 200 points and made it appear that the drop took place over a few seconds—which, if true, would have been really alarming.

TWO AND TWO, NOT ALWAYS FOUR

Odds are the consumers put two and two together—or so they thought—and decided what happened in China was "worse than we thought." So they continued to sell the rest of the day, not realizing until the next day what had happened. This reactive selling was a shame; it was unwarranted and some people lost money. Again this shows once the power of consumers when they choose to react in large numbers causing change as a result. In this case, unfortunately, it wasn't for the best.

Two Potential Keys to Success: Patience and Commitment
Average Annual Total Return: 1985–2006

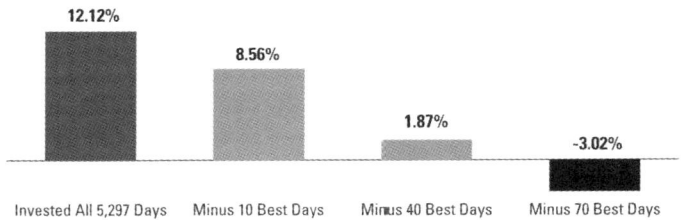

Past performance is no guarantee of future results. The investment return and principal value of an investment will fluctuate.

Source: Goldman Sachs Asset Management.

Furthermore, take a look at the chart above. Notice the time-frame and the number of times if one is out of the market on the best growth days. The average is that missing only two of the best days in the market per year reduces one's return from 12.12 percent to 8.56 percent. Do we really think that we can guess the two best days during an entire year in the market and then just make sure we are invested those days? Are we willing to take that risk? Or is it better for us to stay invested so we don't chance missing them? I'll vote and go with the latter.

REALITY TELEVISION

On a side note, the television reality show *American Idol*, according to AT&T in 2006 alone, received 64.5 million text messages from viewers to vote for viewers favorite "idols." It seems we do want our voices heard, and we value seeing the results of our ability to speak up and affect a result or change in our world. I believe we can take that power and use it for a more important cause or outcome than voting for our favorite new celebrity.

The first example, Halloween, was a negative way that consumers can passionately spread a message. The M&M's example was positive, but perhaps not a very important way that consumers invoked change. The stock market example is a negative example of how consumers react and create chaos and panic. Not very positive, but it reminds us of our humanness and how to fight against it when it causes us to react in a detrimental way for our financial health.

I saved the positive and most compelling story for last.

"IF I DID IT"

In the words of MSNBC contributor, Michael Venture, "About the most disgusting spectacle as had ever been prepared for public airwaves." Apparently, many of us agreed with that sentiment when O.J. Simpson struck a book deal and a two-part television interview to discuss how he would have killed his ex-wife Nicole Brown-Simpson and Ron Goldman. And you and I know most of the general public would have watched, just to see how he acted as he recounted how he "would have" killed them.

I hate to admit that I would have watched. I have taken face reading classes and have studied the art of face reading under Mac Fulfer, who lives in Fort Worth. I would have watched to see what Simpson's face and body language were saying, not just his words. I wouldn't have liked myself for doing it, but no matter how repulsed I was at the thought of the money-making venture, I would have to see what his face and body language had to tell me. I wouldn't have bought the book or spent any money contributing to it. I would have been a supporter of the ban on the sponsors who supported the show.

But I think many of us would have watched it, so it was probably guaranteed to make money.

400,000 BOOKS ORDERED DESTROYED!

There were a reported 400,000 books already printed and sitting in warehouses ready to ship for the November 30 release date. The interview with Fox had been taped and was ready to air on November 27 and 29. In television there is a saying called the "November sweeps," the best episodes are aired at this time and when this week in show business is over, networks are rated as to their popularity. I mean come on, what better time to exploit for profit the death of two innocent people? Fox nixed the show not because it was the right thing to do: it was already produced, remember? And not because they didn't think they'd make money. But because of fear that they would be forever labeled the network that did the "O.J. Simpson" story and the consumer created a popular uprising in which angry citizens voiced their opinion that they would not support this repulsive project. There were even reported boycotts planned of the network's sponsors of the show.

It reminds me of the quote from Thomas L. Friedman's *The World is Flat*, "Sometimes the best way to change the world is by getting the big players to do the right things for the wrong reasons, because waiting for them to do the right things for the right reasons can mean waiting forever."

So needless to say, money had already been spent and "it" had already been produced and ready to generate money. But it was stopped cold on November 21, just six days before the first interview and nine days before the book was to hit bookstore shelves.

WEIRD STATISTIC

So you want to know another reason why I think I'm right and this venture was sure to make money and we all would have watched the show and some people would have purchased the book? Do you want to guess when the most pizzas ever delivered in a three hour period in U.S. history was? You guessed it, the infamous white bronco O.J. Simpson police chase. This is according to a program on the Food Network. Now that's weird!

Now I've been around for a little over forty-four years, and I can't recall an event this monumental, already produced and certain to make money, that was eliminated. The show is canceled, the 400,000 books ready to be shipped for the release ordered "destroyed."

Again, I feel that the words of Michael Venture, MSNBC contributor, say it best, "Finally, sanity reigns. Decency gets CPR. Integrity staggers to its feet. And the power of the people is reasserted."

THANK GOD

Now, thank God that red M&M's are back, and thank God and you as the consumer, that O.J. Simpson's book *If I Did It* never hit bookstore shelves even though a few copies weren't destroyed as ordered (we knew that would happen, didn't we?) I did read somewhere that one original copy that "slipped through the cracks of destruction" went for sale on eBay® for $65,000.

Now since this book didn't get completed before the Goldman family decided to add some text to *If I Did It*, and produce the book for distribution, well I feel compelled to add a few sentences of my own in response.

All I have to say to us the consumer is, "we tried." To the Goldman family, I have never had a child brutally murdered so I can't imagine how that must feel or what it would cause me to do or not to do so to them, I say I hope and trust that you know what you are doing.

IGNORE FINANCIAL PORNOGRAPHY

Now we need to do two things. One is ignore the financial pornography of twenty-four hour news channels and the media, as a way of deciding what to do with our financial lives and investments. Instead hire a financial advisor and make sure they hire professional money managers to manage your money (make sure they ignore financial pornography, most likely they will). When it comes to the media and what they feed us, I have one question for you: If you take their advice and you loose money, can you sue them?

A GRAIN OF SALT

I'm going to let that question sink in a bit. Can you? If you can't sue them for your loss, which you can't, then they aren't accountable for what comes out of their mouths, thus they can say anything they want to, right? In contrast, professional advisors are liable and can be sued for their advise. This is not to say that all news articles, shows etc. are bad: we just have to learn to take what they say with a grain of salt. When you and I do hear something we feel is worth looking into, then we need to call our trusted advisor and bounce the idea off of them, get their thoughts on the idea before we start reacting. After all, we pay them for their advice, so we ought to take advantage of their expertise. I think sometimes in life that as financial advisors, we help people do what is good for them, even when they don't want to. I know my trusted advisors, my CPA and attorney, that is what I rely on and pay them for.

The second thing left that we need to do is to go back to enjoying the fun of Halloween and teach our children the Halloween tradition of knocking on our neighbor's door and saying "trick or treat." Who knows, you and that neighbor may even become friends.

ALL THINGS "RED"
ARE NOT CREATED EQUAL

"As first world consumers we have tremendous power. What we collectively choose to buy, or not to buy, can change the course of life and history on this planet. ... All you have to do is upgrade your choice."
—The (RED)® Manifesto

"There is only one boss—the customer. And he can fire everybody in the company from the chairman on down, simply by spending his money somewhere else."
—Sam Walton (1918-1992)
Businessman and founder of Wal-Mart and Sam's Club

I FOUND "IT" BY ACCIDENT

On one of my monthly trips to Norman, Oklahoma, to see my niece I was at the Sprint store, finally giving in to buying a Blackberry and a Bluetooth earpiece. (I still don't know if the Blackberry is a blessing or a curse, even though I am able to get more done and stay connected to staff, I just have trouble unconnecting now!) There was a pretty diverse selection of earpieces, but there were two that looked identical except for the fact that one was silver and black and one was red and black. The only other difference was the price of the red one was ten dollars more. When I inquired as to what accounted for the difference in price when they looked identical except for the color, the sales representative Chris Schmitz, told me that if I bought the red one, then the extra ten dollars would go to help fight AIDS in Africa.

"REALLY?"

That was interesting to me as I was researching for this book and was all ears. Chris told me that he had written a paper in college about the (RED) campaign. The (RED) campaign was started by Bono, the lead singer for U2, who is also active in charities and influential politics and Bobby Shriver the Yale law graduate who is related to the Kennedy family and very involved in Special Olympics. Chris stated that there were other (RED) products on the market with other companies all chipping in for the cause.

This concept piqued my interest and spoke to the facts I wanted to present in my book. I mean, if we are going to be consumers, which we always will, why not support companies who go out of their way to do good in the United States and abroad by doing exactly what the (RED) campaign set out to do?

PROUD TO BE ASSOCIATED

Now I was already a customer of Sprint, which utilizes Motorola phones among others. Motorola participates in the (RED) campaign. So by accident, I was already a participant myself. Chris told me that the (RED) campaign had gone to other phone companies that were competitors of Motorola and they had refused the (RED) campaign. I was really proud to be with Sprint and Motorola, the company that accepted the challenge. I have to think that you and I are similar and when given a choice, and we know the facts, that we would choose a company that chose to take its political and financial muscle and do something good for the world.

There are many great causes out there for us to invest our time and money in. We are all very busy and most of us won't take the time to do the research to look into charities worth our time and money. So why not let the (RED) campaign do it for us. Bono and Bobby Shriver have already done the legwork. All we have to do as the Manifesto of (RED) states is "... upgrade your choice," and of course choose the products supported by (RED).

INSPIRE SOMEONE

Now I have been criticized for using this as an example because the United States has many causes and issues to deal with and we need help here too. What I say to that is the (RED) program is a great cause, not the only cause but a good one. I hope that this information inspires someone to do a similar program in the United States to help some of the issues we do have here.

HERE IS THE HISTORY

I have become aware of the (RED) campaign by accident through Chris, who generously allowed me to use his paper for research for this book. I was pleasantly surprised and impressed by what I found.

According to the organization's fact sheet, product (RED) is a brand that companies license to sell. Companies whose products take on the (RED) mark make a commitment to contribute a portion of profit from the sale of that product to the Global Fund to finance AIDS programs focused on women and children in Africa. Because businesses also earn profits, the venture is sustainable over the long term.

(RED) was created by Bono and Bobby Shriver. Both also founded DATA in 2002, an organization created to put political pressure on world governments to tackle the key issues surrounding debt, AIDS and trade in Africa.

HERE ARE THE STATS

Every year three million people die of AIDS. Of the 40 million people infected by HIV/AIDS, Africa (which has just over 10 percent of the world's population) is home to 60 percent (25 million). The disease is the leading cause of death in Africa. More than 5,500 people in Africa die each day from AIDS related-illnesses.

Women comprise the fastest growing population group living with HIV/AIDS in sub-Saharan Africa, and the result of their illness on children is compelling. Every time a man or woman is started on anti-retroviral drugs, the survival of children becomes less precarious.

An estimated 13 million children in Africa have already been orphaned because of HIV/AIDS and this number is growing. Almost 2,000 children, most of them from sub-Saharan Africa, are infected with HIV each day. Of the 660,000 children under 15 years old in need of immediate ARV treatment in 2005, 90 percent were in sub-Saharan Africa, according to the World Health Organization.

(RED) contributes to The Global Fund, the world's leading funder of programs to fight AIDS, tuberculosis and malaria. The (RED) contributions do not go to finance tuberculosis or malaria. Since its establishment in 2002, the Global Fund has committed over $7 billion to life-saving programs in 136 countries and accounts for a quarter of the world's funding of AIDS programs in the developing world. Global Fund-financed programs already support 770,000 people on AIDS treatment, provide over a million children orphaned by AIDS with medical service, education and community care, and reach tens of millions with the knowledge and tools to protect themselves against HIV infection.

Additionally, The Global Fund is a lean institution with operating costs of less than 3 percent and is governed by representatives of governments, the private sector, and civil societies from all over the world.

During one week in September, 2006 alone, $4 million of (RED) money flowed to Swaziland. In the words of director of the National Emergency Response Council on HIV/AIDS, Derek von Wissell, "First, a large portion of the money will be directed to orphans feeding them, keeping them in school, protecting them and offering them a future. Second, some of the money will help support the treatment of people on anti-retroviral therapy. (RED) is saving lives. (RED) is helping orphans survive and giving them a better future. (RED) will make a difference.

Companies currently involved in the (RED) campaign include American Express, Converse, Gap, Giorgio Armani, Motorola, Apple, *Vanity Fair,* and *The Independent.*

HERE IS THE BOTTOM LINE

Here are some examples of companies and their products that participate in the (RED) program. Giorgio Armani, Emporio Armani sunglasses, 40% of gross profit margin from sales of all Emporio Armani (RED) products goes directly to the Global Fund.

- Converse, Mudcloth shoes, 15% of net retail sales goes to the (RED) campaign
- Motorola, (RED) Motorola SLVR, 5% of Net retail sales, starting from $60. Additionally, if you buy the SLVR from a Carphone Warehouse, Motorola adds another dollar for a total of $10. As soon as you use your SIM card in the red MOTOSLVR, your network detects that you are using a (RED) phone. For as long as you use the handset, your network will donate 5% of your mobile phone bill to fight AIDS. (A gift that keeps on giving).
- *The Independent,* United Kingdom's publication, contributes 50% of the day's revenue to the (RED) campaign May 15, 2006
- Giorgio Armani, Emporio Armani watch, 40% off gross profit margin
- *The Independent,* All revenue from online sales September 21, 2006
- Apple Inc. iPod nano Product (RED) Special Edition, $10
- Motorola, (RED) Motorola RAZR, $17
- Apple Inc. iTunes Product (RED) Gift Card, 10%
- *Vanity Fair* magazine, June 2007 issue, $5 of every subscription to *Vanity Fair* sold

The feeling these companies get from doing well and the feeling we get for doing the right thing? Priceless.

All you have to do is go to www.joinred.com, click to get registered and fill in your information. It's free. You will then have an account that will track all of your (RED) purchases and show you what those purchases bought for someone in another part of our world. You can become a part of something special, big and powerful. Besides, it's the (RED)... I mean... right thing to do.

BY THE WAY...

That ten dollar contribution that I made when I bought my Bluetooth? It bought 20 single-dose (nevirapine) treatments for mother and baby to prevent the transmission of HIV from mother to child. All by becoming a little educated one Saturday and making the simple decision to "upgrade my choice."

I Have a Vision

"I have a dream."

—**Martin Luther King (1929-1968)**
One of the main leaders of the American civil rights movement
and Nobel Peace Prize winner

"The deepest principle in human nature is the craving to be appreciated."
—**William James (1842-1910)**
Influential psychologist and philosopher

So this adventure we've been having may seem a little too idealistic for you. After all, an idealistic concept called The Human Factor used as a way to market and grow your business? Come on. But when I say I have a vision, it is a vision of the companies in our world doing exactly that.

After all of my research, and talking and reading about highly effective business leaders and business owners, I have come to a conclusion on how a company can take all of the attributes of The Human Factor and create what I call a vision for the future. A company is highly effective and successful not in spite of The Human Factor but because of it.

IF YOU GO

When you are in Fort Worth, there is a company that emulates The Human Factor. Now it won't be a sightseeing trip like the Fort Worth stockyards or the many museums the cultural district has to offer, but if you just take I-35 south from downtown a few miles, and ask for a tour of one of our most esteemed companies—Alcon Laboratories—you'll see what I'm talking about.

After you visit Alcon, I have to think that you, like me, will be extremely impressed and you will understand why an entire chapter is warranted and why I see them as a future vision for all companies.

I have to say, a few years ago I formed an early impression of the character of Alcon executives when I heard Jackie Fouse, at the time CFO of Alcon Laboratories, speak at a local business function. Her obvious passion for Alcon and what they do to help the less fortunate around the world was captivating and contagious. That talk several years ago planted the seed for me to want to research to see what exactly caused such enthusiasm and what made Alcon employees tick.

THREE PRIMARY MARKETS

Alcon has three primary markets, surgical, pharmaceutical, and consumer products. Surgical is primarily the treatment of cataracts. Pharmaceutical encompasses glaucoma and eye diseases. Consumer products include contact lens solutions and dry eye products.

There are United States and international product managers in each of the three areas. Alcon has entities in seventy-five countries, not including the individual distributors located in remote countries.

Alcon's goal is to design products in the United States, create a brand for the rest of the world and create affiliates with key people and physicians around the globe who can champion, lead, and implement their global strategy.

The areas of the world that Alcon targets are the United States,

Latin America, CAFE (Canada, Australia, the Far East), Japan and EURMEA (Europe, Africa, Middle East).

A COOL STORY

Alcon Laboratories was founded in 1945 by two pharmacists in Fort Worth, Texas. They combined the first syllables of their last names, Robert Alexander and William Connor, to create the name Alcon.

Today, Alcon is majority owned (75%) by Nestle S.A. and incorporated in Hunenberg, Switzerland, with the United States operation based in Fort Worth. Alcon has 13,500 employees worldwide and their development, manufacturing, and distribution of eye care products reaches 180 countries.

In March 2002, Alcon underwent an initial public offering on the New York Stock exchange. In 2006, Alcon's sales reached nearly five billion dollars.

INTERVIEWS

I interviewed two leaders at Alcon to give you a perspective on a few specific areas of the company. The Director of Humanitarian and Community Services and the Senior V.P. of Global Manufacturing for technical operations. I hope these interviews help you understand how Alcon markets, how Alcon gives back to humanity and how Alcon produces its products. All of these play an important role in making Alcon one of the most well-known names in the eye care industry.

ATTRACT TALENTED EMPLOYEES
AND HIRE THE RIGHT PEOPLE

Alcon's reputation often precedes the employees that go to work at the company. The reputation the company has built actually attracts talented employees.

Employees often comment on how empowered they feel at Alcon. They feel empowered because the company listens to their ideas and encourages their feedback. Employees also feel they are given the right tools to do their job.

People who do business with Alcon often comment on the company using words like honesty, trustworthy, punctual, straightforward, ethical, non-aggressive, easy to work with and friendly, all words used to describe this exceptional company.

As I talked with Alcon employees, I was reminded of my own theory of the best employees: ones who act self-employed. They really take ownership and have enthusiasm for their work, and they would be self-employed if it weren't for lack of resources or the security of the backing of a large corporation. They truly love what they do.

HEART AND SOUL

They put their heart and soul into it, and it shows in their work. This is partly due to their personality, but they have to find a place to work where their expertise can be valued, and where they can be allowed to grow, listened to for their ideas, and given the right equipment, tools and technology to do their work. When all these resources are in place, these people are unstoppable and the companies that hire them are enriched way beyond the expense of their pay.

HIRE DIVERSITY

For Alcon to be competitive in foreign markets, they realize they need to hire people from different cultures and countries who will be sensitive to the needs of the various people from diverse walks of life. Also, people in foreign countries appreciate it if you can and do speak their language, even though English is spoken in many countries. This cultural awareness is where many companies miss the boat, as they don't have their employees take the time to learn about the culture of the country or learn to speak another language, which places them at a disadvantage. Alcon gets this part of doing business in a global economy and seeks out diversity to help it market products in all parts of the world.

Interestingly enough, of the eight clients at Alcon that we help in our financial advising firm, one is from Turkey, one from Spain, two are from Canada, two from India, and two from Texas. That is pretty diverse within just those eight!

PARTNER WITH THE RIGHT PEOPLE

Alcon creates strategic alliances with the leaders of eye research, diagnosis and treatments from all over the world. They identify people in the eye care industry who are setting standards for treatment and collaborate with them. Many of these people are at universities where they teach but have a private practice as well. In ophthalmology for example, it is a hands-on profession where people wanting to do research are studying and seeing patients.

In addition, Alcon realizes that the company can't do everything in-house. It needs partners in foreign countries and universities to help them on projects. In return, Alcon might give these individuals personal grants for their own projects. I have to think that because of this win-win situation, those people are advocates for Alcon Laboratories.

LISTEN TO YOUR EMPLOYEES

From talking to Alcon employees, it is obvious Alcon provides an environment that has been open and responsive to ideas. This causes employees to feel they are being listened to and feel that they can make a difference in the company. Furthermore, if an employee gets bored in his or her current position or just wants to try something else, there are different careers within Alcon that employees can do, another reason why employees stay committed and stay at Alcon.

LISTEN TO YOUR CUSTOMER

Alcon is good at involving the customer in what they are doing, sharing information with them, and learning from them. Alcon asks customers if a product or tool would be beneficial to the people in their country. By doing this, Alcon keeps their customers engaged and in contact with them and encouraging their feedback.

AGAIN, ALCON'S REPUTATION IS KEY

Ed McGough is Senior V. P. of Global Manufacturing and Technical Operations. With an engineering degree, Ed began his career as a quality engineer at Baxter. Ed first learned of Alcon while he was at Baxter as Alcon made surgical products that Baxter used. Ed had visited Alcon a few times while working at Baxter, and his visits formed an early impression. In 1987, Ed's boss at Baxter left to go to Alcon. Four years later, with encouragement from his old boss, Ed followed suit and joined the Alcon team. Ed's commitment to Alcon is evident as he was willing to relocate to Puerto Rico for three years after one and a half years at the Fort Worth plant.

After his work in Puerto Rico, Ed was able to come back to Fort Worth, which is home for him and his family. Ed is responsible for all of Alcon's manufacturing plants around the world. Two are in Fort Worth and there is one each in Spain, Belgium, France, Brazil and Mexico respectively.

When I asked Ed what made Alcon a great place to work, he replied, "They have an attractive and safe campus to work in. They produce ethical pharmaceutical products and medical devices. They have a very diverse market and products." He compared Alcon to a well-diversified investment portfolio where there are several asset classes. While some may be doing well, some may not, but the net affect is steady growth through good times and bad. Ed feels this makes a career at Alcon very secure, not to mention their buy out by Nestle, in 1978.

It certainly doesn't hurt to be bought by a large global company. I can appreciate that as our financial advising firm was bought by a large global player as well, and both Ed and I benefit from these buyouts through our respective stock benefit packages.

STABILITY IN LEADERSHIP

Ed also shared that he valued the stability of Alcon's leadership. When employees see long-term leaders, it gives them more job security and reinforces the culture in that organization and does not promote change for the sake of change. Usually, when management in an organization changes, the new management implements their preferred business model, which is often different. Having longevity in leadership creates continuity. Ed said that most CEOs today stay at a company on average only four years.

That makes sense to me and reminds me of a recent headline that left me scratching my head in wonder of companies in this country and their incentives. The headline went something like this: CEO leaves after two years with a multimillion-dollar settlement. Ok, let me get this right: so the individual who was the CEO for a short time failed so they gave him this huge settlement that is more than enough for several of us to split and retire on? Where is the incentive to do the right thing, grow the company and then be rewarded for the growth? I certainly don't get that logic.

LISTEN TO EMPLOYEES

Ed continued that employees see security in leadership. The employees need to buy into the leadership's business model, vision, and strategy so they will want to execute it. Not for fear of losing their job if they don't, but because they believe it in their heart. Ed believes employees and managers mirror the personalities of their leaders. At Alcon, the leaders are socially oriented and very approachable. Employees are listened to and encouraged to give feedback.

Another point that resonated is how critical it was to empathize with the employees, listen and try to understand why an employee or a team is underperforming. Ed encourages these discussions and keeps his own ego in check by listening to what they have to say and waiting to see what solution they come up with on their own. He states that amazingly, when given the initiative to collaborate on their own, they come up with a similar solution, as he would have suggested. It is better when they come up with it themselves because then they own it, and they are the ones that are going to go back to their team to implement it. He only makes suggestions after they have come up with their own conclusions to maybe tweak the idea or challenge them on why their idea may or may not work to help them think it through.

EMPLOYEE EMPOWERMENT

Ed said that when management allows employees this kind of empowerment, they in turn value their leader more, because they were given the freedom to solve their own problem and in doing so increased their own self-worth and confidence. This kind of leadership also creates a culture of self-sufficiency, resulting in a more efficient operation and one that actually needs less of Ed's time and attention.

CHAT SESSIONS

Ten to twelve times a year, Ed and his team hold what he calls "chat" sessions. These are sessions where no management or human resource representatives are present. He rotates the employees who attend and keeps the group around ten people to further encourage open feedback. To make sure all are included, he pulls employees from both the first and second shifts.

The meetings begin with the positive question, "What do you like about working at Alcon?" Someone in the group takes notes, and management sees if there are some consistencies in the feedback trying not to make changes in what employees like about working at Alcon. Then the meeting changes to "How can we make Alcon better for you?"

In one meeting an employee brought up the fact that at one end of the manufacturing floor the lighting hurt his eyes and made it hard for him to do his job. Ed went to investigate and discovered that the lighting was very different in this area of the floor and could empathize with the employee's observation. The cost for new lighting was $20,000. In a few days, the lighting was replaced. The next time Ed saw the employee, he told Ed how thrilled he was with the new lighting and how he appreciated Ed listening and making the needed change.

Ed stated that this kind of emotional bank account creates a loyalty that employees don't want to disappoint their leader or manager, and so work harder on their jobs. We all want to be seen as important, and we all want to feel valued. Ed creates that environment and eventually changes the culture for the organization in a positive way. The emotional bank account that Ed refers to is more important during bad times than good times when you are more likely to see it pay off.

TREAT EMPLOYEES LIKE CUSTOMERS

This story reminded me of another story about the owner of the Dallas Mavericks basketball team, Mark Cuban, who reportedly went to the highest seats in the new American Airlines Center and asked those customers how they liked the new arena. One fan told Mark that it was great, but in the corner seats he could not see the clock, and that if the clock had another side to it, he could see the score from his seat. Mark looked up from where the fan was sitting and realized one couldn't see the clock from that angle. Mark went out and bought a new clock with two extra sides, so the very next game the clock could be seen by fans in those sections.

I'm sure that both Ed and Mark created loyal and passionate fans in both their employee and customer alike.

EMPLOYEE WELLNESS

Alcon promotes the wellness of its employees. Each employee is encouraged to participate in 30 minutes of exercise each workday, and to log on to the virtual fitness program that Alcon has implemented.

While I was listening to Ed, it occurred to me that all of these factors are a big reason why this large international company still feels like the little company that started 60 years ago in Fort Worth, Texas.

Make Employees Accountable

According to Ed, it is important to hold employees accountable once employees are given a task. You can hold people accountable in a militaristic or dictatorial style, or you can get people to do things because they don't want to disappoint you. If people make improvements just to advance their career or to not get fired, those motivating factors create a negative culture.

Ed reasons that most people are inherently good, hard-working people. They really don't want to call in sick when they are not or lie to management. They want to feel important and valued. If you encourage them to do the right thing, empathetically listen to their concerns, try and take action on those concerns, apologize when you make mistakes and show you are human, more than likely they will want to please you and will make the better choice. You and your company will benefit by the positive and efficient culture you have created.

GIVE BACK TO HUMANITY

Ed said that Alcon not only gives back to humanity, but encourages its employees to do so as well. Ed is involved in Junior Achievement, the United Way, and Prevent Blindness Texas.

He feels proud to be a part of an organization that gives back to the community. Thanks, Ed, for your great insight into Alcon's leadership culture and your insight into leading people the "Alcon way."

STARTED AS A SECRETARY

We all love rags to riches success stories, don't we? That is probably one reason reality television shows have been so wildly popular over the last decade. We love to root for the underdog, and if we can't progress into a better life, we love to see it happen to some other ordinary person. Maybe that is one reason most of us are eager to help others advance when we have the power to help them. So when I interviewed the director of Humanitarian and Community Services and she told me she started as a secretary at Alcon, I loved that!

1,100 MISSION TRIPS A YEAR

I am speaking of Winona Edwards who started her career at Alcon as a secretary reporting in to Corporate Cash Management in 1986. At that time, the supplies for the medical mission part of Alcon were stored in a small room . The mission program had humble beginnings in 1963 fulfilling a request for two-dozen units of glaucoma products, which were all stored in a broom closet. Today, Alcon participates in 1,100 foreign medical mission trips a year and responds to more than 36,000 requests for glaucoma products for needy U.S. patients every year. The total units of Alcon products donated today exceed 400,000 each year.

When Alcon started its medical mission support in the '60s, the medical ship "Good Ship Hope" was well known as a medical community for doctors who wanted to donate their time and skills. One of the doctors called cn Alcon to see if the company would be interested in donating the needed supplies to help them complete their planned mission effort.

An observation I made during our interview was the pictures that line the walls of Winona's office and meeting room. She certainly can afford fine art to decorate her surroundings but that is not what you see on the walls. Her walls are lined with photos of Alcon's supported mission trips, and the people in the photos almost tell you a story and speak to you as you look at them. These are all photos of Alcon helping the less fortunate in the poorest parts of our country and abroad.

WORD-OF-MOUTH

Alcon's involvement in missions really started via word-of-mouth (not the first time we've heard that idea). About the same time as Alcon partnered with the "Good Ship Hope," SEE (Surgical Eye Expedition) and other eye health care non-profit organizations started as well. These organizations started from the realization of the eye doctors visiting developing countries and learning that one of the primary needs in these remote areas was the removal of cataracts. The simple removal of a cataract took a totally blind person from blindness to sight virtually instantly, which was very dramatic and rewarding for the eye doctors and the patient to experience.

CONTAGIOUS ENTHUSIASM

This visible transformation the visiting doctors witnessed created a contagious enthusiasm because in developed countries like the United States, the cataracts would have been removed more than likely before total blindness set in. This enthusiasm spread, and more and more companies like Alcon became involved as well as the doctors needed to perform the procedures. They were and are equally dependent on each other. The doctors cannot perform the surgery without the supplies and equipment, and the suppliers like Alcon cannot facilitate the use of the needed supplies without the doctors to administer them; a great partnership that makes a lasting difference in the lives of those who make the surgical procedure possible, and for the individuals who have their sight restored.

Alcon's philosophy is as long as there are eye care professionals who donate their time in the mission field, Alcon will contribute the needed medicines and surgical products. Many doctors even come right out of college with the idea of donating a part of their lives to medical missions. This is amazing to me when you think about the personal debt that doctors incur in schooling.

SKILL EXCHANGE

The host doctor for the country can see the opportunity for a skill exchange with the visiting doctors. The doctors participating in the mission also benefit as they see diseases in more advanced stages than they see in the United States, which helps them better understand various diseases.

The missions use whatever they can safely convert in the local town they are visiting to the "hospital" that would serve them during their stay. A tent to an old school, to a pop-up trailer or anything else that might be converted, was made sterile and used as the mission's hospital.

These mission trips might encompass a team of from four to sixty persons with the normal stay for the team of two weeks. All team members pay their own expenses. It is also common for doctors to go the first time with the established charitable organization on their own. Then, finding the trip to be so rewarding, the second visit often includes their spouse or entire family. The experience these teams receive is humbling and creates gratitude for the richness they realize they have in their own lives. Egos are kept in check as they all serve a common goal with no personal agenda.

PERSONAL EXPERIENCE

When I asked Winona to recount her most memorable trip, she told me of the trip she took as a part of Medical Ministry International (MMI). Alcon was the main supplier of medicines and surgical equipment for providing eye care for this trip, which took them to La Esperanza. They flew from the United States to San Pedro Sula, Honduras. Once in Honduras, they boarded an old rickety bus and drove five and a half hours to La Esperanza. Interpreters from the local high school stayed with the doctors, nurses, and the team. There were local cooks who assisted the North American volunteer cook to prepare daily meals for the team, which helped make them feel welcome.

There is an MMI office in El Progresso, where the team first checked in upon arrival and met the in-country organization personnel that would help carry out the mission in the mountainous region near La Esperanza. It was very important for the locals to be involved so it would not be seen as the North Americans coming in providing care and leaving. As an added benefit, the local physicians who participated in the mission were able to study under doctors from a developed country. The experience created more self-sufficiency and a better understanding of treatments that were provided.

1,500 TO 2,000

The first day of the mission, 1,500 to 2,000 people lined up to receive care. Many walked two and three days to get to the makeshift clinic. The only form of communication for these people to know about what day to show up to receive treatment was via word-of-mouth. There were only specific days that eye treatments would be given, and it seemed like a small miracle to Winona that the people who needed eye care came on the correct day.

THEIR "SUNDAY BEST"

Winona was also impressed that the future patients were so quiet, waiting patiently for their turn in line with no complaining. They were also dressed up in their "Sunday best" to see the doctors. This is not surprising when you realize that seeing a doctor in a remote region may happen once or only a few times in their entire lifetime.

I can imagine that these doctors were seen more like gods than people. Patients who were totally blind when they walked in one side of these makeshift clinics would emerge from the other side in less than an hour with an eye patch on. The following morning at post-op, the doctor removed the patch and they were able to see. With family members standing by, the smiles and tears from the patients, relatives, doctors and all the volunteers was an unforgettable experience. No interpreter was needed to clearly understand the joy-filled patients—some whispering, some crying aloud—"I can see you"

One of Winona's most moving moments was when a mother and her beautiful sixteen-year-old daughter, whose eyes were crossed, came to the clinic. The girl was visibly sad. In this culture, the mother knew her daughter's visible physical impairment would keep her from marrying and meeting a future mate that could possibly help her advance in life. (In third world countries remember, for women, marrying a "provider" is often the way to a better more financially stable life.) The morning after surgery at post-op examination, daughter and mother embraced each other, tears of happiness running down the little girl's face along with a great big smile as she was handed a mirror to see her beautiful brown eyes perfectly aligned for the first time in her life.

Some of the people who stood in the long lines to see the doctors had no visible signs of impairment. Winona discovered that these people just wanted to "see" a doctor, and the fact that they could see one made them feel better.

LARGEST SUPPLIER
OF OPHTHALMOLOGY PRODUCTS

With Alcon's participation through product donations supporting volunteer surgeons' charitable efforts, in foreign countries more than 25,000 people a year are treated for cataracts alone. ORBIS, an organization with the world's only flying eye hospital, has received support from Alcon since its inception in the early '80s. Alcon donates 60 percent of the ophthalmic supplies ORBIS utilizes in its educational programs on the plane and in the off-plane programs. Alcon is the largest contributor of eye care products for Mercy Ships, a United States based non-profit organization with a fleet of hospital ships off the coast of Africa and around the world. Eye care is a big part of their mission through their Mercy Vision program.

MISSIONS AREN'T JUST
FOR FOREIGN COUNTRIES

Every year in the United States, Alcon participates in assisting more than 30,000 United States citizens in their Patient Assistant Program.

During the interview, Winona's colleague Kathleen Golden shared that she came to work at Alcon based on her passion for eye care treatment. Kathleen's mother and father have ocular hypertension, her brother has glaucoma, and her grandmother has wet age-related macular degeneration. What better place for her to work than a company who is solving eye diseases and creating solutions to treat eyes? Alcon is a company that visibly shares its knowledge and products with those less fortunate. Because of what the company is known for, Alcon creates passionate employees who are advocates for the enterprise in which they work.

14,000 PAIRS OF GLASSES

Another Alcon mission Winona joined was in Morocco with the LensCrafters Give the Gift of Sight program. The LensCrafters mission team took 30,000 pairs of glasses sorted by prescription. In seven days, more than 14,000 people were examined and matched with a pair of glasses to use.

For this mission trip, there were twenty-five volunteers and the makeshift clinic was in an old school compound.

Again, Winona was struck by how quiet and orderly the people were, especially when one morning they arrived for clinic and one thousand of them were children. All were crowded around the entrance to the school compound, anticipating their turn. As the twenty-five volunteers came toward the crowd of roughly two thousand, the crowd parted, making a path through the sea of people so the volunteers could enter the clinic area and start their work. As the volunteers passed, the crowd of children started clapping with their small hands and cheering. Winona said the entire team was humbled and honored to be a part of such a rewarding medical mission that was obviously appreciated by this gracious group of people. It was also remarkable to Winona that the people never asked for food or water as they waited patiently for their turn, especially the children.

The only disheartening part of the trip was when the staff and the crowd realized with only a few days left of their trip, there were many who would not be able to have their eyes examined. They would have to wait until another mission team arrived.

CAN YOU SEE IT?

Can you see what kind of world we'd live in if companies created businesses like Alcon?

Can you see why I call Alcon a vision for the future?

GREEN EGGS AND HAM
AND OTHER "FUN" STUFF

"Say I like green eggs and ham! I do like them Sam I am. I would eat them in a boat. I would eat them with a goat. I do so like green eggs and ham. Thank you, thank you, Sam I am."

—**Dr. Seuss**
Green Eggs and Ham

"Two roads diverged in a wood, and I took the one less traveled by, and that has made all the difference."

—**Robert Frost (1874-1963)**
Mountain Interval, 1920, *The Road Less Traveled*

HAVE YOU NOTICED?

As we travel the roads and highways of this great country of ours, have you noticed that the towns we journey through are all starting to look the same? As we pass through towns, we see the same chain stores one right after the other as if we were stuck in a bad movie or a mad version of "Groundhog Day," because we keep seeing the same thing over and over again. Because these chains are taking over our towns, the mom and pop small businesses are becoming few and far between. We are losing culture, character, community, and yes an aspect of humanness (The Human Factor) when we allow this to happen.

Now, I consider myself a realist and I do patronize chain establishments. At the same time, I am ever conscious of supporting local establishments in my own ccmmunity and other communities when I travel.

BESIDES...

According to a publication by the *Door County Compass*, March 27, 2006, recent studies show that for every $100 spent at a chain retailer, only about $13 stay in the community. But when that same $100 is spent in local stores, $45 stay in the community. That equates to over three times the amount of money put back in the community. That is a scary and an obviously detrimental statistic that we all need to keep in mind when we decide whose doors we walk through to spend our hard-earned money.

A CURTAIN

Consider those easy access chains, shops, and restaurants that line our freeways as a curtain covering up the real gems of shops and restaurants that our towns have to offer. More than likely you will have to travel past the curtain of shops along the freeway to see the real treasures awaiting you. In our financial planning firm, we work with small business owners. Our hearts go out to those hard working individuals who are trying to make a living, and who are giving us something special and unique in return.

Local stores bring character, community, and humanness to our lives. In addition to all of that, quite frankly, they also bring us more fun and interesting lives. One of the interesting things that I find is having the chance to meet the owner or talk to an employee who knows the story of how or why an establishment was created.

There will always be an interesting story for sure—stories like the business being passed down through generations, or the owner who experienced life in the corporate world and witnessed inefficiencies or realized there was a better way to do business, and treat employees and or treat customers. In a sense, from most of the businesses I encounter, the individual's drive, ambition and ideas are created from the desire to do business better, but also add back The Human Factor that often gets lost in corporate America.

To help motivate you to support local businesses and discover the gems in your own town, I've included a few stories I have collected along the way.

GREEN EGGS AND HAM

I'll bet you're like me and when you read the quote for this chapter, you smiled as you read those familiar words from Dr. Seuss. Now it isn't so much that you would ever order green eggs and ham—part of the fun of it is that you could have. When my niece or granddaughter are old enough to appreciate it, I do plan to take them to Yogi's Deli and Bagel Cafe for green eggs and ham. The fun for me of course will be watching them experience something that no one, when reading the familiar Dr. Seuss book, thought they would ever actually be able to order somewhere, someday.

How cool is that?

THE DINER

Since I travel north to Norman, Oklahoma, once a month to see my one-year-old niece Brooke, my sister-in-law Rose, and my brother Barton, I get a chance to visit one of my favorite restaurants in Norman. The Diner is similar to one you might find off the beaten path in your hometown or in your travels across the country.

On a recent visit, as we sat at the Diner's counter, I watched my one-year-old niece be totally entertained for at least twenty minutes as she watched the cooks make pancakes, eggs, and hash browns as the grill is exposed for all to see. As I watched her be amazed, I started to become impressed myself with the way the cooks orchestrated the cooking process as if they were creating art. This is not a fancy place by any means, but as I watched them move as they cooked, their arm movements and the way they knew where each other were and the waitresses grabbing the freshly prepared food just at the right time– it really did flow like art. The space that they have to work in is very small so each step does have to be orchestrated so no one runs into each other. It is just pretty amazing how they flowed and moved together.

A sign above the grill reads "Mark Sez Food is Love. Have all the love you can handle!! Leave the rest...It's OK."

Great advice, Mark!

TOMMY'S, THE BEST DARN HAMBURGERS IN FORT WORTH

When *Texas Highways* magazine went on a search for the "best burgers in Texas," naturally Tommy's was on their list. Their search exhausted the entire state. After tasting Tommy's burgers, the magazine ranked Tommy's hamburgers the third best burger in the entire state.

Tommy's has a standing position with our local newspaper *The Fort Worth Star-Telegram* as the "critique's choice" for burgers. In 2005, *Fort Worth Texas Magazine* ranked Tommy's as the best burger in Fort Worth. Tommy's also had a long run of "best burger award" with the local paper *The Fort Worth Weekly* newspaper, from 1998-2005.

5-CENT HAMBURGERS

You read that right. On Tuesday nights, at one of Tommy's locations, they have 5-cent hamburgers. You buy one at the regular price and you get the second one for a nickel. So take a friend so you can split it, which is more fun anyway. right?

FERNANDEZ CAFÉ: MEXICAN FOOD
WITH A DASH OF HEALTHINESS

I found this marvelous place by accident and it is less than a mile from my house in Fort Worth. I found it over ten years ago, and I'm still a big fan. I can grab low-cal breakfast tacos on my way to work or swing by after work and have a "Rick bowl." This heart-healthy dish was actually named after a local cardiologist who asked the owner one day to make something special for him. He said he wanted boiled chicken with cilantro and whole beans with rice on the bottom and lettuce and tomato on the top. It is very tasty and healthy at the same time. Healthy Mexican food—who says you can't put those three words together?

The low-cal breakfast burritos have whole beans, potatoes and egg whites in a small tortilla so they are relatively healthy as well. And since it is really my home away from home with cooking that tastes homemade, it's a good thing it is healthy too. When I feel like some home-cooked food, since "home-cooked" at my house is a rarity, it is nice to have a place to run to when I feel like having food made from scratch. When you walk into the restaurant, on the right side by the kitchen door, there is a large round table where all the regulars sit when they are dining alone. You feel as if you are a part of the family and that you are always welcome, especially if you are dining alone. It is comforting to know there is always a seat waiting for you when you arrive. The hospitality of the Hispanic population is very welcoming and I never really thought about comfort food before, but at Fernandez I do feel comfort from the home cooked dishes. Also, the way this culture makes food celebratory is refreshing. At Christmas, Betty and her crew are very busy making at least 100 dozen tamales made to order, a Mexican and Texas tradition.

The hot sauce is awesome. Enrique makes two different kinds fresh every morning. This is a place that makes Fort Worth feel like a small town. If you are a regular, you can even set up a tab and pay when it is convenient. Now, how many places let you do that?

NO ONE NAMED "NORM"

The regulars all know each other, usually just by first name. There is no "Norm" like on the "Cheers" television show, but there is a Rick, a Bob, an Alan, a Charles, a Tom, and a Gene. Meré and Christina are the regular waitresses that have been there since I can remember. You can catch up on local happenings and the latest news in the paper or on the television above the pop machine. And if you stay awhile, you can usually help solve at least one of the problems going on in the world.

GOOD FOOD

In a one time contest in 1994 to discover the best enchiladas in Fort Worth, Fernandez Café won three of the four enchilada awards and beat out eighteen of Fort Worth's best Mexican restaurants. Cheese enchiladas are one of the many foods that I continually research in local restaurants to see who has the best of the best. So even though I know that was a few years ago, don't worry, I've been continuing to test them and they are still on top.

We all have a human need of feeling a belonging, of community and it's nice to walk into a place knowing there is a chair for you and a place where many people know your name and inquire as to what is going on in your life. Fernandez Café is one of those places like I hope you discover in your town.

Thanks Tony, Betty, Enrique, and Jamie for creating a home away from home.

WELCOME TO THE NEIGHBORHOOD—
THE NEIGHBORHOOD GRILL

Normally, when you enter The Neighborhood Grill in Fort Worth, you are greeted by Peter Schroder, the owner who celebrates ten years in business this summer. Peter picks up bits and pieces of his customers' lives by inquiring about their children, grandchildren, recently taken vacations, and so on. Each conversation may only be a few minutes, but it is a snippet of their lives and Peter has the uncanny ability to remember the last conversation he had with a particular customer and pick up where they left off from their last visit. In my last book *Tattoo*, I discussed how we all have the desire to feel special, and this owner certainly makes his patrons feel special when he remembers the people and the events in his customers' lives and then asks about them on their next visit to his restaurant.

As you might have guessed, the grill is off the beaten path of the highways of Fort Worth, so you will have to take the road less traveled to get there. But you will be pleased and pleasantly surprised by the hometown feel, friendly atmosphere, and great food.

Thanks, Peter, for creating a family friendly, and neighborly establishment worth writing about.

PIRANHA'S: KILLER SUSHI

I moved to Fort Worth in 1985, and the only way I would have been able to eat sushi back then was to drive east to Dallas. Partly thanks to the Bass family bringing the renowned 61 million dollar Bass Performance Hall to Fort Worth, our city has truly expanded in terms of culinary cuisine offerings. Of course we have more chain restaurants now, but we also have restaurants owned by entrepreneurial individuals. Piranha's sushi restaurant is one of them.

In fact, if you are longing for sushi, the best sushi west or east of the Trinity (sorry, Dallas) is Piranha's. The sushi is not just the best tasting but also the best presentation, as every dish offers a beautiful display of culinary pleasure.

LIFE'S A BEACH:
MAKE A SAND CASTLE WHILE YOU WAIT

How fun is that? At Life's a Beach, you can kick off your shoes, grab a sand bucket and shovel, and see what you can build while you (and your kids can too) wait on your dinner. The play place at McDonald's has nothing on this restaurant!

The bar in this establishment looks similar to your average sports bar. Nine plasma screen televisions line the walls. But there are a few novelties: you can sit at surf board tables, and there is a life-size shark that apparently burst through the outside wall—his mouth open wide, holding a flat screen plasma television for your viewing pleasure.

A few clients of ours are regular patrons and one couple believes enough in the restaurant that they are investors.

GRADUATE OF CIA
(NOT YOUR TYPICAL SPORTS BAR FOOD!)

Jim Verfurth, the forty-six-year-old restauranteur and owner, is not new to the restaurant business by any means. A graduate of the Culinary Institute of America (CIA) in New York City, he was an employee in a large restaurant for several years before branching out on his own ten years ago and starting The Village Grill in Highland Village, Texas, and Celebrations Grand Ballroom.

A FAMILIAR RING TO IT

Jim's reason for leaving the corporate world has a familiar ring to it. When the ownership of the corporation changed hands and went from the father to the son, the focus of the company's mission changed and Jim did not like it. Jim's philosophy was take care of the customer and you will make a good living. The company's focus became spending money on upgrading office furniture and unnecessary frivolous items that were really for management, not the customer. The company had even done a study prior to the ownership change that estimated each customer was worth $42,000 in a revenue stream over their lifetime.

RITZ CARLTON

This reminded me of the Ritz-Carlton's study I discussed in my first book *Tattoo*. Ritz-Carlton guests account for a revenue stream of $250,000 over each guest's lifetime. We can all apply this to our own businesses and determine what our customers are worth. No wonder studies show us that it is much more cost effective to retain existing customers than to gain new ones. Just this year, we evaluated our customer base and determined this client dollar amount for us as well. This is not a bad exercise for businesses large and small to gain a perspective on what customers are truly worth. Knowing how much our customers account for on the bottom line ought to encourage us to treat them well.

LEFT BECAUSE OF UNDESIRABLE CHANGE

Change forces us to reconsider our options, put things in perspective and help us realize what we do or don't want in life.

So when Jim saw a shift in priorities from the customer to what is best for management and stockholders and the goal became to create an initial public offering of stock to share on the open market, Jim knew it was time for change.

He realized he was taking a chance branching out on his own in a business that is highly competitive and that has a high failure rate. Yet he believed he could create an experience for his customers that would be successful by being a smart businessman and taking care of the customer. After ten years, I'd say it was a good decision for him.

He has not one but four restaurant ventures adding to his obvious resulting success.

I am only discussing one here, because it was the one I was

introduced to initially. And even though all success stories are fun to me, the Life's a Beach theme seemed like the most fun story.

CREATING SOMETHING UNIQUE

Since I had the opportunity to visit the restaurant prior to our interview, I had already made some observations, one was what I call the cool crushed ice "let me hold your drink while you wait" trough. When I asked Jim about it, he told me it was actually called a "frost rail" or "frost top." Several years before "Beach" was created, Jim had seen one at a pub in Ohio. He had told himself that if he ever had his own bar, he would have one of those. This attitude and drive is a very likeable quality of Jim's and it resonates with me as well. It is a quality that makes you want to create the best thing possible in life, and when you see something you want to do, don't just talk about it, do it!

Jim also shared with me that when he told the designers for the restaurant what he wanted, they hadn't seen one and had no idea what he was talking about. I asked Jim, "Didn't you just love that? That what you want is so unique that people have rarely seen them, let alone have them!" I'm always excited to hear about something special and unique. And that is exactly what will cause others to go out and talk about it, because it is rare and special. The creator, in this case Jim, went out of his way and spent extra money to deliver that experience to his customer.

A PASSION FOR THE ISLANDS
(CALLING ALL PARROT HEADS)

The idea for Life's a Beach came from Jim's partner Scott Richardson who enjoys traveling to the islands around our globe like St.Thomas and the like. The name dictated the concept and the theme developed around the name. The deck for the restaurant was designed and built first because outdoor dining was the initial concept not an afterthought. The concept is that once customers walk in, "the rest of the world goes away" just as if they were on vacation. You can't see traffic or even a parking lot through any of the windows, all you see is a beach with a city park in the background. All your cares go away as you listen to island music. If you are a "parrot head" you will be pleased as you often will hear Jimmy Buffet music.

KIDS CAN BE KIDS (NO FIDGETING HERE)

The other attraction for parents and kids alike is the beach that allows kids to be kids while waiting on dinner, and parents not having to tell kids to not fidget in their chairs or tell them to quiet down as they are playing in the sand while awaiting dinner. So it is a bit of a vacation for parents as well and how much more relaxing can that be? Interestingly, when I asked about the many sand buckets and shovels that are by the deck for anyone to grab, Jim said, "We have never bought a one of them." He explained that families come to have birthday parties for their children and the consistent party favor is a sand bucket with a shovel. As parents really don't want to take them home, they leave them so others can enjoy them. Jim also mentioned that it is a regular site to see a family walk in with a few children with them and you guessed it, they come prepared with their own bucket and shovel to use while dining, which often get left as well.

NO MORE DINNERS IN A BOX, THANK YOU

"Beach" was also inspired by Jim's personal experience as he and his wife were married for eight years before having children so were quite used to dining out. After the children arrived, to keep them occupied while dining, he said his life became food in a box at local chain restaurants with playgrounds for kids. He thought there had to be a better way, and better food too! I can imagine with a degree from one of the finest and well-know culinary schools in the country, his palate would cringe at the food from the average fast food chain.

What about the food? The menu is one of the most extensive menus I have ever seen, and with my lifestyle for the past twenty years, almost every meal is at a restaurant or brought home from one. The two dishes I have had were excellent. I viewed plates of others, which had great presentation and looked equally great as well.

Thanks for a great and fun concept, Jim, and for giving us high quality, relatively quick food, and not in a box! I can't wait for my next trip to Highland Village, to try out another of Jim's creations.

IT JUST SEEMED ODD

Sixteen years ago, while in Philadelphia on a layover, leaving the classes I had taken at the American College in Bryn Mawr, Pennsylvania, I spent my last night in Philadelphia and was directed by the hotel concierge to a restaurant called the White Dog Café.

When I enrolled in a retirement planning class at The Wharton School at the University of Pennsylvania in 2007, I found myself in Philadelphia, Pennsylvania, once again. One of my business partners, James Taylor, was going with me and one of our clients, Steve Schack, loves Philadelphia, so before we left Steve gave us three "must see" restaurants to visit. When James showed me the list, I couldn't believe that the White Dog Café was one of those three. Now I have to admit I really was done with this chapter, but when James directed me to The White Dog Café's website, what I found spoke so well to the message of this book, I felt compelled to include it.

HISTORY

The White Dog Café opened in January, 1983, as a take-out coffee and muffin shop on the first floor of Judy Wick's house at 3420 Sansom St. The menu soon expanded to soup and sandwiches, which were made in Judy's upstairs kitchen. Soon, there was a grill out back, where hot food was served and seats were added in the backyard where the porch was built later.

As I was reading the history of The White Dog Café, I was reminded of how similar it was to a Fort Worth institution, Joe T. Garcia's Mexican restaurant. More on that later.

One glance at the first page of the White Dog Café's website tells you much about what this establishment stands for. There are four areas on the site to click on and research what is important to the owner and what she stands behind: serving customers (have to love that concept because it is what my last book was based on), serving our community, serving each other, and serving the earth.

A LITTLE HELP FROM HER FRIENDS

When capital ran short at the beginning of the White Dog's existence, according to the website "... luck was with us and a loan from a friend provided the capital to install the indoor bar, grill kitchen and bar counter which opened in the spring of 1984, but the basement floor was still earth and the public restroom was still upstairs in Judy's house." Construction of additional dining rooms and kitchen areas followed from 1986 to 1997. In April, 1989, The Black Cat Store, a gift shop, opened next door.

Judy has won many awards from 1991 to 2007. She won the National James Beard Humanitarian Award, the only one in the entire country in Judy's field, and the Philadelphia Sustainability Award for her lifetime achievement and honoring her career in Philadelphia for positive environmental and social change.

MY SECOND VISIT

On my second visit, we arrived about 2:30 in the afternoon and were famished so we decided on a late lunch and early dinner. I had planned to visit the White Dog Café before the trip was over, but I didn't really have in mind when I would go. James and I went to the concierge for advise and the first words out of her mouth were, "Your best pick would be the White Dog Café." That settled it. We were glad we did as we found out they actually have five different menus depending on the time of day you visit. So you really get a wide variety early in the day, mid-afternoon or evening.

After reading the history on the website, and realizing how Judy's enterprise had almost everything to do with what I was writing about, I had to pick up a newsletter at the front door and see what else I could discover from tidbits on the menu.

"BECAUSE I LOVE ANIMALS"

When I asked Judy what inspired her to go into business, she caught me by surprise when she answered, "Because I love animals." I told her she had totally lost me on that response. She explained that when the restaurant went from coffee and muffins to serving full menus, one item she had to start purchasing was meat. She wanted to actually visit the company that provided the meat. How many restaurant owners do you think care or take the time to do that?

Judy continued that what she had found at the slaughter houses repulsed her. She realized there was a humane way to kill animals and these companies were not doing it.

She decided that if she had to buy meat she would only do business with companies that treat the animals humanely. That is standing up for what you believe in and staying committed to your convictions even if it costs you more time and money—you have to love that in a person.

BUY LOCAL AND IN AMERICA

One paragraph on the drink menu summed up one of the ideas for this book in White Dog perspective: "The White Dog serves only American beer because beer is best when served fresh, without the preservatives necessary for travel and storage. We are committed to building the local economy by buying from locally owned companies which also cuts down on carbon emissions caused by long-distance shipping." On other literature entitled "Where does our food come from?" another sentence reads, "We are also committed to supporting the local economy and focus our list on locally crafted beers." I really liked the way they stated that and also that their signature "Leg Lifter Lager," is as pleasing to my palate now as it was sixteen years ago.

In the literature at the door to peruse while dining, there is a list of the suppliers and farmers that supply the White Dog Café. They are truly making themselves accountable for supporting the buy local idea.

WHITE DOG WISDOM

This interesting information is taken directly from the White Dog literature. "The first project of the White Dog Café Foundation (now White Dog Community Enterprises), the Philadelphia Fair Food Project, is dedicated to bringing locally grown food to the Philadelphia marketplace and promoting humane, sustainable agriculture in the Greater Philadelphia region. They connect farmers with wholesale and retail markets while connecting consumers to food grown in the region. Fair Food programs include resource guides of local farm products, education and advocacy work around humanely-raised animal agriculture, a weekly farm stand, and fun events related to food and farming. For info on Fair Food projects or to join the mailing list, please visit the Fair Food online at www.whitedogcafefoundation/ fairfood.html." Additionally included in their literature is a website www.buylocalpa.org to see where local food outlets are located.

When Judy put her purchasing philosophy together for her hand-outs, she stated her mission eloquently. "By choosing food grown locally by family farmers, you are supporting a lifestyle that respects and protects the earth. Humane and sustainable agriculture produces wholesome food in a manner that is sensitive to our ecosystems, compassionate toward animals, and provides a safe environment for present and future generations."

Well put, Judy!

FORT WORTH ICON

It would probably be considered unethical by local Fortworthians to not include Joe T. Garcia's if I'm going to talk about local restaurants. There is an entire book written on the history of this restaurant, including the family that started it, so I'll only briefly mention its history.

The Joe T. Garcia's story starts out very similar to The White Dog Café's history. The grandchildren of the original owners now run the restaurant. If you go to the restaurant, it won't be hard to tell what part of the restaurant was the original home of the Garcia family. Joe Lancarte's grandmother would make home made tortillas, burritos and tacos. The milkman and mailman would be on the north side of Fort Worth making their daily stops stopping by at just the right time to savor fresh cooked food. They would be invited into the Garcia home to sit at the kitchen table, now still the entrance to the restaurant, and eat the homemade food. Her husband who worked at the old Armour Swift packing plant, also on the north side by the stockyards, would take to work homemade food to sell to his co-workers. These activities and word-of-mouth spread around Fort Worth and the continued success of great quality, good tasting Mexican food has now become a Fort Worth icon. The original home is the cornerstone of an enterprise that now stretches a full city block complete with a garden to host outdoor quincean~eras and weddings. A parking lot almost as large as the facility itself is across the street to accommodate customers.

IN GOOD COMPANY

Twenty years ago, I worked out at a health club at the same time as one of Joe T. Garcia's grandsons, Joe Lancarte. We were part of the 6 a.m. club so we had a chance to get to know each other. He would come work out and mention certain celebrities that had been at the restaurant. Since it is in the stockyards in Fort Worth, close to Billy

Bob's Texas, the world's largest honky tonk, country music artists like Garth Brooks would be regular patrons. Other celebrities went there to try out the legendary haunt—Michael Keaton, right after he had done Batman, and Michael Jackson reportedly flew in to town, ate at Joe T's and flew home. When you go there, there will be photos of celebrities around the restaurant, and depending on your taste, you'll be in good company.

NO NEED FOR DIRECTIONS

Twelve years ago, when we started doing informal educational and fun events for our clients, Joe T's was a natural fit. When sending out invitations, there really was no need for a map to Joe T's let alone an address. If you go on a Saturday, prepare for a good wait after 6 p.m., sometimes up to two hours. But people don't seem to mind as they chat with each other. If nothing else, the people in line all have something in common: more than likely, they are there because they love Joe T's.

Joe T's also gives back to their local community with the annual run to Joe T's event benefiting The Samaritan House. Do you remember the statistic that of $100 spent at a chain establishment only $13 goes back to the community, and when a $100 is spent at a locally owned business, $45 goes back to the local community? I hope you will consider that statistic when you contemplate whether to spend your money at a chain or local establishment.

NO MENUS

By the way, there are no menus because there are two things on the menu: the family style enchilada dinner of two large cheese nachos (my favorite), two enchiladas, two tostadas, rice, and beans; or fajitas, choice of chicken or beef. This is one of the endearing things about the restaurant in my opinion, and one more thing that makes it unique.

Thanks, Joe, and the rest of the Lancarte/Garcia family for making a Fort Worth icon that we can be proud to support. We will continue to be proud of your high quality food and your giving back to our community. We know you will do your part on keeping this legend of ours, Joe T's and Fort Worth on the map.

REATA: ROPE IN SPANISH

The Reata restaurant is probably one of the most popular restaurants in all of downtown Fort Worth, serving weekday lunches of 250, weekday dinners of 350, weekend dinners of 800. Reata has a total seating capacity both indoor and outdoors of 550, spread over four stories. Weather permitting, outdoor dining for about 150 is available year round. On the fourth floor there is an outdoor bar, indoor dining in a geodesic dome for about 90 and outdoor dining for about 60 on the sunset deck. Reservations are taken, but there are always seats left so that walk-in customers can be accommodated.

Reata is named after the ranch in the classic 1950s movie "Giant" starring James Dean, Rock Hudson, and Elizabeth Taylor. Reata's owner is Al Micallef, although in the past Al has had partners Mike Evans and Grady Spears.

TORNADO DESTROYS ORIGINAL LOCATION

In March of 2000, a tornado ripped through downtown Fort Worth, reportedly staying on the ground for an estimated 100 miles. The tornado went through downtown Fort Worth, fortunately around 6:30 p.m. Had it been an hour earlier with most of downtown still alive with many people in their offices, the death and injury toll would undoubtedly have been higher. Still the tornado did cause severe damage in many homes and office buildings, but only one reported death.

LEGENDARY WESTERN CUISINE

One of the hardest hit buildings was the Bank One building in downtown Fort Worth. The top floor was home to the original Reata restaurant location and one of the most splendid views of the downtown skyline as well as out west to the prairie of Weatherford and east toward the skyline of Dallas. People came from all over to experience the views and the unique cuisine. My favorites are the many salads and the tenderloin tamales, and, of course, the ever popular dessert tacos with caramelized bananas and the Dutch oven apple crisp with cajeta, a Mexican caramel. Its menu is self-professed legendary western cuisine. It is a great place to take a touring guest for unique options like duck, or quail and other delicacies.

My suggestion to you is come visit our wonderful city, make Reata one of your stops and whether you eat upstairs or not, take the time to tour the restaurant to see the unique room on the bottom floor as well as the roof top bar. If you don't think you'll ever make it, Reata has a few cook books on the market, if you'd at least like to replicate this fine cuisine at home.

After the tornado, the restaurant struggled as "what to do about the damaged Bank One building" was up in the air for literally two years before Reata secured a new location in the old Caravan of Dreams.

After being forced out of the Bank One building and its 35th floor perch in February of 2001, it took Reata 15 months before it was able to open its new location in the old Caravan of Dreams in May 2002.

FAMOUS SKYLINE VIEW

But what to do about the ever popular views that had been on top of the 35th floor of Bank One? The now former Caravan of Dreams location is only four stories tall with buildings all around it with little opportunity to have a skyline view. What do you do? You hire a local artist. In this case, the Reata owners hired local photographer Rhonda

Hole. The photos are floor to ceiling panoramic photos replicating the view from the 35th floor of the Bank One building. The room is titled the "tornado" room and a memento case in the hallway displays the remains of a champagne flute and leather menu cover in the spirit of a Titanic memorial. Reata was able to keep one of its reasons for popularity, the view, regardless of the fact that it wasn't on the top floor of a 35-story building but rather in the basement of an alternative location.

MOST DESTRUCTIVE TORNADO IN U.S. HISTORY

When the dust settled and Reata reopened in its new location, it can claim that it survived the most destructive tornado in United States history to date according to Reata's website.

I chose Reata, because it is so west, so Fort Worth: a popular meeting and eating place for locals and tourists alike. The owners are sticklers for buying locally when they can—their beef, furnishings and so on. If they can't buy local they certainly buy in Texas. What I discovered, however, goes beyond that and speaks to the heart of The Human Factor, by how the company treats its employees and gives back to the community.

KEEP YOUR NAME IN FRONT OF YOUR CUSTOMERS

The owners are smart business people. They did a great job of keeping the Reata name in front of their customers while it struggled to find a new permanent home. They created Reata on the Road, a catering venue, and Reata at the Rodeo, a 56-seat full service restaurant inside of the Amon G. Carter Exhibit hall, which is home to one of the largest rodeos in the country, the Fort Worth Live Stock Show and Rodeo. After the experiment of trying Reata at the Rodeo, it has now become a consistent dining venue every winter in January and February when Fort Worth hosts one of its biggest events, the Stock Show and Rodeo.

In 2002, Reata added its own line of food items under the name A Taste of Reata. One of the initial offerings was the tenderloin tamales, which were sold in local grocery stores and retail outlets. The line has subsequently expanded into other states.

In 2008, Reata took over the Legendary Backstage Club at the Fort Worth Stock Show and Rodeo. The club operated as a private club during its first year. It has had overwhelming support from the community and when it cut off membership sales because of capacity, it had over 150 people/companies on the waiting list.

GIVING BACK TO HUMANITY

Reata gives back regularly to the community via Meals on Wheels, Cancer Care Services, the WARM place, American Cancer Society, the local Jaycees, the Fort Worth Zoo, and the Western Heritage trail. Western Heritage trail is a self-guided walking tour of downtown Fort Worth as well as a collaborative community program to call attention to famous people and places of Cowtown. Whether it is a donation of catering services for charities to raise money for the charities or of proceeds from the Reata cooking school, several charities in Fort Worth have benefited from Reata's charitable Human Factor interests. Also Reata is involved with All Church Home, National Cowgirl Hall of Fame, Fort Worth Chamber of Commerce, "Braded" and celebrity cutting benefitting the Careity Foundation.

TAKING CARE OF EMPLOYEES

What impressed me the most as I researched this unique establishment was how it took care of its employees who—without an actual work location—would obviously not be receiving paychecks for awhile. Co-owner Mike Evans said, "Just because the building is closed, doesn't mean our employees won't get paid. I met with employees right after the tornado and let them know that they would have continued employment with us." He explained that they would continue to pay some of the 150 employees to work for the American Red Cross, helping the victims of the tornadoes in Fort Worth, Arlington, and Grand Prairie. "We are going to set an hourly rate for anybody who has to continue to work to be able to pay their bills," Evans said. Those who did not work for the Red Cross were offered a temporary job at JMK Management Corp., owned by Reata co-owner Al Micallef.

The restaurant closed for 42 days. When the restaurant was ready to re-open, the owners brought everybody back. The management and employees worked seven days a week, twenty hours a day to reopen quickly. Reata was the only tenant in the building for almost nine months before it was forced out of its majestic location. Amazingly during the nine months in a severely damaged building, Reata's sales continued to increase.

I had the opportunity to talk to Mike Micallef, who is Al Micallef's son and is instrumental in Reata's success. Since Mike became involved with Reata in 1995, he has put teams together that have created a 60 per cent increase in sales. Mike feels the success of Reata has to do with the quality of the teams that are in place.

Mike shared with me that when Reata announced to the community that they were going to have to close the restaurant, with no idea of when they would be able to re-open, he told me that Reata received overwhelming community support. The support was evident when after the Thursday through Sunday following the announcement of the restaurant closing, Reata had its four busiest days ever.

Mike went on to tell me that many people came to reminisce about times they had at Reata, from birthday parties or special dinners at Reata where men had proposed to their current wives.

Now that is a company that cares about its employees, takes care of them in ways that obviously cost them money, and gives back to humanity at the same time. No wonder I wanted them to be featured in this book!

Thanks Al and Mike Micallef, for a true story that's worth telling, and writing about but not just by being a great example of our western heritage and a great place to take out of town guests, but a great example of how when we treat our employees well, and do the right thing as humans by giving back, we can create a successful business.

WORDS OF ADVICE

When owner Al Micallef was asked in an interview in November of 1998 by the *Star-Telegram,* for "the best way for a small or new company to build a reputation in its industry" he responded, "By always keeping your word and doing what you say you will do. Deliver on time, pay your bills on time, and make sure they know you kept your word. Build that credibility, because most companies won't do it. It's not anything malicious. It's just that things just fall apart most of the time."

IN MY LITTLE WORLD

Of course, these places just happen to be places in my little world, but no matter where you live you have a Tommy's or a Neighborhood Grill, so patronize those establishments.

Now I'm a realist and I know some chains are individually owned through franchising. And I know when you and I are short on time we will go through the drive-through for that quick burger. And I'll bet that most of these chains will survive in our towns because of that.

But we need to support our local establishments when we can. It is getting harder and harder for the small business owner to compete with the big chain establishments. When you are out of town, when you have time, go off the beaten path and discover local shops that are unique and privately owned. Find out from a local the best place to get Mexican or Thai food—most likely it will be off the beaten path or freeway, but I'll bet you'll be rewarded for the extra effort after you experience these places.

BESIDES...

How fun is it to feel like we are trapped in a really bad movie anyway?

CONCLUSION

"The call and need of a new era is greatness. It's for fulfillment, passionate execution and significant contribution."

—Stephen R. Covey
From *The 8th Habit: from Effectiveness to Greatness*

"That a man can change himself...and master his own destiny is the conclusion of every mind that is wide-awake to the power of right thought."

—Christian D. Larson (1866-1954)
Influential new thought leader and teacher

WHAT I HOPE

As an employer, you motivate employees to be more efficient and better workers. Challenge them to be the best employees they can be for you and for themselves, and then reward them when they accept the challenge. This positively impacts their own lives as well as your business which will not only cause them to be better workers for you and improve their efficiency and quality of work, but will reward them with a higher quality, more fulfilling life as well. Create a company worth someone talking about and spread your message by being fair to employees and customers. Give back to humanity, and you'll do well by doing good.

IN A NUTSHELL

As a consumer, buy local when you can. Support those hard-working entrepreneurs in our towns and support businesses that do the same. Think of it like the Red campaign—upgrade your choice by doing business with the companies that value The Human Factor. We can affect change when we feel it is warranted. We can do the right thing and make a difference. The end result is that we can make our place a better world in which to live. Don't forget about the tremendous power we have as consumers to affect change. Hey, we got red M&M's® back, didn't we? And O.J. Simpson's book never hit bookstore shelves (well, almost didn't).

THE TIME HAS COME...

...to test ourselves.

Whether it was a few hours ago, yesterday or last month when you started this book, take a minute to take this short test. Come on, it will be fun. More importantly, you can rate both of us: me on how well I was able to get my message across to you and you on how well you retained it. As I said early on, I wanted this to be more than you just reading a book, I wanted you and me to have an experience together.

By the way, the longer it has been since you read various parts of this book, the harder it will be for you to complete this experience and recall what I shared with you throughout the book. And you know why don't you? You took your child to the doctor. You had a not-so-fun discussion with your mother-in-law. You returned one hundred and ninety-nine emails and deleted that many more. You fired your lawn guy. You found a new dentist. You went online to find out just how much your insurance was going to pay for that dental procedure you've been needing. And... you potty trained the dog that the family "had" to have.

So with all of that chaos since you've read the various chapters, just as you need to get your message across to your customer, I had to give you information worthy enough of being remembered, and the only way to know how successful you and I have been along this journey is for us to test ourselves.

Rank yourself on your ability to recall and my ability to give you something memorable to forever change the way you look at marketing, and the way you market your message or business today.

Let's see how we did:

MAKE BELIEVE
- What was the technician's name in this chapter?
- What were the two most threatening aspects of the virus?

INTRODUCTION
- Recite two lines of Ring Around the Rosy and recall their meaning.

THE HUMAN FACTOR
- Name one of author Barbara Ehrenreich's jobs as she went undercover as a $6 an hour employee.

THE TEN ATTRIBUTES OF THE HUMAN FACTOR
- Name two attributes of the Human Factor and provide as much detail as you can about it.

YOU GET WHAT YOU PAY FOR
- What company is this referring to?
- Do you do business with this company?

HALLOWEEN, RED DYE NO. 2, AND O.J. SIMPSON
- What do these three things have in common?
- Recount the stories that sociologists believe attributed to the "razor blades in apples" myth.
- Why did people stop buying M&M's?

ALL THINGS "RED" ARE NOT CREATED EQUAL
- What does this chapter tell us about our power as consumers?

I HAVE A VISION
- What is the primary treatment Alcon Laboratories provides to third world countries and why is it so rewarding to doctors and valued by patients?

GREEN EGGS AND HAM AND OTHER FUN STUFF
- From this "buy local" chapter, name one restaurant featured and what made it memorable to you.

Answers begin on the following page.

Here are the answers.

MAKE BELIEVE
- The technician's name is Seth Daniels.
- The two most threatening aspects of the virus is that it is airborne and there is no known cure.

INTRODUCTION
- "Ring around the Rosy" speaks to the fact that one of the symptoms of the disease was a red ring that would appear on the body of the person afflicted.
- "Pocket full of Posies" referred to the myth that if a person put rose petals in a pocket it would ward off the evil spirits that gave them the plague.
- "Ashes, Ashes" referred to burning the bodies in the streets to try to keep the plague from spreading.
- "We all fall down" references the fact that "we all die," as 85 percent of those afflicted died of the disease.

THE HUMAN FACTOR
- Barbara Ehrenreich's jobs were, a waitress, a maid, and a Wal-Mart employee.

THE TEN ATTRIBUTES OF THE HUMAN FACTOR
1. Invest in The Best Technology
2. Hire The Right Employees
3. Hire Diversity to Market Globally
4. Listen to Your Employees
5. Hold Employees Accountable
6. Think of Your Employee as a Customer
7. Provide a Good Environment for Your Employees to Grow
8. Listen to Your customer
9. Give Back to Humanity and Encourage Your Employees to as Well

10. Create a Story

YOU GET WHAT YOU PAY FOR

Gotcha, I'm not going to tell you the name of the company I referred to in this chapter so no points for either question, but I do think you are probably smart enough to figure it out.

And I hope I at least made you think twice before you do business with them again in the future.

HALLOWEEN, RED DYE NO. 2 AND O.J. SIMPSON

- These three things all remind us of the power we have as consumers that when we want to cause change by our actions, we can. It also reminds us of how powerful word-of-mouth communication can be when we repeat stories. Whether they are true or not, they can spread across the country and amazingly last decades.
- The stories that the sociologists believe caused the "razor blades in apples" myth, was the child who overdosed on heroin and his family sprinkled his Halloween candy with heroin to cover it up. The other story was of the father who tainted his child's candy with poison to try and collect on an insurance policy the father had on the child.
- People stopped buying M&M's because the government came out with a publication stating Red Dye #2 was harmful if ingested and consumers erroneously believed that Red Dye #2 was used in making red M&M's.

ALL THINGS "RED" ARE NOT CREATED EQUAL

- This chapter reminds us of the power we have as consumers to vote with our checkbooks and be conscious of where we spend our money.

I HAVE A VISION

- The primary treatment that Alcon Laboratories provides for their missions is the removal of cataracts. It is so rewarding for the doctors and their families because in the third world oftentimes the cataracts are so advanced that the patients are totally blind. The removal of the cataracts results in a totally blind person being able to see, often within only an hour.

GREEN EGGS AND HAM AND OTHER FUN STUFF

- Restaurants in the chapter were: Yogi's Deli, The Diner, Tommy's, Fernandez Café, The Neighborhood Grill, Piranhas, Life's a Beach, The White Dog Café, Joe T. Garcia's and Reata.

Scoring: *Five points for every correct answer, a possible high score of 70.*

Score 0-15—I probably need to consider not writing another book.

Score 20-45—Okay, but maybe I should be a co-author.

Score 50-70—Hey, maybe you and I are on to something here.

Well, hopefully we earned a high score together. Thanks for taking this journey with me and I wish you all the best in spreading your message, in your business, and in whatever you have set out to create. May you prosper more than you have in the past, and at the same time make this world of ours a better place to live.

ABOUT THE AUTHOR

"Some people enter our lives and leave almost instantly. Others stay, and forge such an impression on our heart and soul, we are changed forever."

—Unknown

"There are essentially two things that will make you wiser, the books you read and the people you meet."

—Charles Tremendous Jones
Known as one of the most dynamic speakers
in our country over the last fifty years

Just so you know, what you are about to read has nothing to do with business and what you have just experienced.

If you read "Tattoo," and you have already read this section, I'll save you some time: skip to page 154 for an update on my life since 2004.

EVERYONE HAS A STORY

I am not writing this because my story is so important, but because everyone has a story and this is mine. I feel compelled to share my story with you for three reasons. One is that my life is not so exciting that one day someone will want to write my biography. So I figure over the next few pages is my only chance to tell my story. Secondly, I consulted many clients, friends and local authors on this journey I've had of writing. And many of them encouraged me to write about my life. So here it is, and for those of you who encouraged me, I have one thing to say, "Be careful what you ask for."

Third and most importantly, I hope that this will motivate you to write your own story. Homer Hickman, author of memoirs and other fine books, states, "There are stories inside each of us that wait like magic spirits to be released from our hearts." And Frank P. Thomas, who wrote *How To Write Your Life Story,* and who has read thousands of manuscript pages of people's lives, states that he has "seen an instinctive urge deep in the heart of people to learn more about who they are and where they come from." He calls personal memoirs "a precious document that can live in your family for generations."

I'm sure there is someone in your life that will appreciate your taking the time to write about your life. And certainly no one can tell your story like you can.

BEING ADOPTED

I was born in Topeka, Kansas in 1963. My biological mother was twenty-two and unmarried when she had me. I would later learn why she gave me up for adoption. She didn't know my father, and she felt in her words that I had a "better chance at life" if I could grow up with both a mom and a dad. She also said she didn't think it was right or fair of her to keep me.

Coincidentally, at age twenty-two, I decided to contact her for one main reason, to tell her "thank you" for having me. I imagined through her life she had wondered to herself if she had done the right thing by putting me up for adoption. I wanted to assure her she had. I had a wonderful life with my mom, dad and brother and sister.

I contacted the Kansas Children's Service League to find out how to contact my mom. Their policy was that they would look in my file to see if there was a forwarding address for her. If there was, then that meant she wanted to be contacted, if there was no address, then she didn't. Fortunately, there was an address.

You often hear stories of people searching for years and spending all kinds of money trying to find their parents. Well, I guess I was lucky. Within a week, I received a letter back from her. And when I got to the bottom of the letter I had to smile; she signed her name, "Dorothy." But what other name would she have had, to be the mother of a little girl who grew up in Kansas and was living for the most part, a fairy tale life?

She told me in her letter how she thought of me every year on my birthday, which surprised me. I wasn't around to remind her of the day and to celebrate it. So I never once considered that she would remember my birthday. I think that made me feel special.

She sent me a photo and described herself as 4'11" with black hair and sharp blue eyes. Her heritage was French, American Indian, and Irish. Of course, that is only half of my biological story, and I have to admit that I was a little disappointed when she told me that she didn't know much about my father. She only said that he was athletic, muscular, good looking, and apparently, irresistible.

EVERYTHING HAPPENS FOR A REASON

We never did meet, and unfortunately I have lost her information. But I do believe everything happens for a reason. She told me after reading my letter that she knew her prayers had been answered and that she had made the right decision by giving me up for adoption. It made me feel good that I could help her be at peace with this decision she had made in her life.

"YOU'RE ADOPTED?"

My mom and dad kept a storybook that described how they "picked" me out and took me home. At the end of the book was a photo of me. They were so matter of fact about it, that I never wondered much about "adoption" until attending school and kids would say "You're adopted?" with surprise in their voice. Their questions about it always surprised me. The way my parents explained how they adopted me seemed so normal, and I accepted it as such. They told me how they went to an agency, kind of like a store, and picked me out.

My sister had been adopted two years before me, so for a long time adoption was the only way I knew how you had children. It wasn't until kids questioned me about adoption that I started to wonder about it. If you aren't "picked" out, how else do you show up in life? So even though they explained to me what adoption was, I didn't know how it was different than how everyone else arrived here in the world.

In the early '60s, adoption was not as common as today, and some parents who adopt would choose not to tell their children about the adoption. It was a little taboo and somehow I think society felt sorry for parents who "had" to adopt, because they couldn't have their own children. To make it "easier" on the parents, agencies would often try to match eye and hair color of the adopting parents to the baby. In fact, both of my parents had blue eyes and dark hair, as I do.

MY PERCEPTION OF THE WORLD

I guess for most of my life, and maybe this was the start of my perception of the world, I've felt the glass is half full, not half empty. I figured being adopted was a good thing. I mean, someone didn't want me and then someone did. So that's a wash, right? How is that bad? To this day, there is a special place in my heart for people who adopt. Besides, if my parents had to pick me out of a baby line up, I must have been the cutest and best looking baby for them to pick me over all of the others. I think this gave me a healthy ego, and it also was one more thing in my life that made me feel special.

MY MOM'S INFLUENCE

Growing up, my mom made it very clear that there was a wrong way and then my mom's way of doing things.

She was meticulous about our home being clean, very organized and always presentable in case someone would drop by unannounced.

My mom was also adamant that we were properly dressed for whatever the occasion and she taught us to take pride in our appearance.

In my mom's world, everything had its place in the house and I could retire now if I had a dollar for every time she told us "put things back where they belong."

Being a little opinionated and a little stubborn are traits my mom and I have in common. And since we didn't always share the same opinion, a conflict between us would often arise as a result. Because she felt so strongly about many of her beliefs, she would challenge me on my views when we didn't agree. I realize now that this actually helped me form my own opinions and beliefs by defending them. It made me realize what I did believe in, and I am very thankful for her influence.

I have more discipline, more determination and a strong sense of what I believe in because of her. I'm not the most organized person you'll ever meet, but I'm less disorganized because of her influence on my life.

Because of my mom, birthdays were highly celebrated and the person with the birthday was made to feel special. We were able to choose themes for our birthdays, which often would include an elaborate and detailed cake to match the theme.

Breakfast, lunch and dinner at our house were always with us seated around the dinner table. It is interesting the effect I now know that had on my life. At a square or round table you sit directly across from someone, which makes it easy to look them in the eye and talk about the day's events or whatever was on your mind. From others' accounts of growing up, I'm not so sure that this practice was or is the norm. But I think it was good for us, as it helped our family talk more and it gave me a feeling of security and stability.

My mom was very strict about the amount of television we were allowed to watch. She called it the "boob tube." We were allowed thirty minutes each day. And on the weekend or special occasions we might be allowed longer. When she would leave the house for an errand she would take a tube from the back of the television to insure we wouldn't watch it while she was gone.

I certainly don't win at television trivia games but I'm thankful for her limiting our viewing time. My brother and I spent more time outside playing and interacting, which was good for us. My sister chose to spend her time reading and as a result, she is an avid reader with a large vocabulary.

FOND MEMORIES AND PHOTO ALBUMS

Our home wasn't the only thing that my mom was detailed and organized about. My brother, sister and I all have several complete photo albums and scrap books. These albums detail the place and date of birthdays, band trips, vacations or other life events that she wanted us to have a memory of.

My parents believed in the family vacation. Every summer we would pack the station wagon full of food for the road and beam in anticipation of what we were going to do and see on our trip.

Without CDs, cassettes, eight tracks or MP3 players, the radio was about all there was to listen to and I remember that it didn't work very well, anyway, so it was usually turned off. To pass the time, we would sing songs, often hymns that we knew from church, or play road games that my parents made up.

Most of us probably have a "story" that our parent repeatedly told about us that was their favorite. For my dad, mine must have been when we were on a family vacation, I was a few years old and we were at the hotel pool. I was sitting on the edge of the water, my dad was close by but I managed to jump in and proceeded to sink right to the bottom of the pool. My dad quickly went down after me, pulled me up and sat me back on the side of the pool. Since I had swallowed water, I was coughing and spitting it up in attempts to breathe. As he was getting out, still spitting up water I promptly jumped right back in. Needless to say, my dad felt it best that we go back to the room. My parents recognized my fearless and unpredictable nature and realized they would have to keep a close eye on me.

My parents knew they were building memories for us and I believe that was their intent. I know they sacrificed by doing the things that would be fun for us, but not necessarily fun for them.

My father loved Colorado so that is where we went most summers. When I was twelve we started going in the winter too so we could snow ski. We would stay in condos that had kitchens. I remember my mom making casseroles for breakfast and dinner. She would freeze them, pack them in the cooler and even put the date the dish was to be served on top of each container.

My father was very involved in the Kansas Savings and Loan Association. As a result he would often travel. Wherever he went, even on short trips, he would always bring something back for us. I would get excited about something as simple as the pens with liquid and a floating object inside of them. I thought "how exciting to go and visit different cities."

My dad would also bring me a bar of soap from the hotel where he had stayed. At the time, the hotels would have a drawing or picture imprinted on the paper that wrapped the soap. I don't know why I kept them but I had a large shoebox full of soaps that I kept into my adulthood. Maybe they were little reminders of these exciting places he had been and a reminder that he thought of me and made me feel special.

As a child I thought, "If I can't do what he did for a living so I can go to exciting places then I'll be a truck driver." In my little mind, I thought that would be a good way to "see the world."

I also remember in second or third grade when the teacher asked us to each state what we wanted to be when we grew up. I remember saying a "millionaire." Everyone laughed, but I was serious. Obviously at the time my ambition for wealth (so I could do whatever I wanted whenever I wanted), and my career choice didn't necessarily match.

THE MIDDLE OF NOWHERE

Most of my life growing up was spent in a small town in the middle of nowhere in Kansas; Lyons, Kansas, to be exact. I call it the middle of nowhere because if you wanted to go to the mall or a movie, you were in the car for an hour to get there.

To further illustrate the meaning of the phrase "the middle of nowhere," in a travel book I highly recommend, *Road Trip USA*, the author describes a highway that goes right through the middle of the state and thus through the middle of Lyons. It is US 56, and the author labels it "the loneliest road in America." I think you get my point. There are, however, two stop lights as you pass through on highway 56, so you won't necessarily "miss it," but it is a small dot on the map.

"THERE'S NO PLACE LIKE HOME"

There is openness to the sky and countryside in Kansas that I actually miss. In fact, it is funny how I thought I would never miss the openness of the country, but I do. And now that I live in Fort Worth, if I drive an hour in the right direction, I can see openness that reminds me of home. It is interesting that growing up we would drive an hour to "be" somewhere, and now I enjoy driving an hour to see nothing but countryside and sky.

Now that I think back to when I was young, we would spend many a night sitting on the back of my dad's car looking up at the sky, especially on stormy nights. The openness in Kansas causes you to instinctively look up as you walk outside. I heard once that more native

Kansans are in the aeronautical field than from any other state.

Not that Fort Worth is a huge city, but the sky does get lost with the lights of downtown and the buildings that are there.

My dad was a banker, and I suppose we were considered upper middle class in the tight knit community of Lyons. We were members of the nine-hole grass green country club (I say grass green because in the smaller towns there were actually sand greens and you had to rake the sand on the green, after you finished putting on them). So we all thought we had something special, with our country club with grass greens. Many people were members of the country club just for the social membership, so they would have a nice place to eat on Saturday night without needing to leave town.

RANDOM THOUGHTS

For some of us, those sixty-thousand random thoughts that scientists tell us that we have each day are more often and more random. Looking back on my elementary school days, I never really excelled in school. I think my teachers would continue to pass me because I did show up for class. However, paying attention when I got there was another story. My parents even took me to a specialist to find out why I didn't do well in school. He was at a loss after my examination. I'm sure I had and still have attention deficit disorder. I'm also relatively sure, from the stories, I am the hyperactive type.

Of course they didn't know what to do with that disorder at the time, nor did they even know what it was. So I learned to adapt, but school was always hard for me. Even though I know now, of course, that I am intelligent, at the time the way teaching and testing was done, and with my attention problem, the results appeared as though I wasn't intelligent.

It took me years to get over my insecurity and to realize I was actually smart; it just didn't seem that way at the time. Also, as a child when an adult tells you something, you accept what they say as the truth without challenging them. So I bought in to what I was told by adults, that I just probably wasn't going to be able to do much, because I was a "little slow." I was told to not expect to go to college and to try and find something I enjoyed, that wasn't going to require much schooling past high school.

EDUCATION

I did finish my bachelor's degree at Kansas State University in '85, and in '94 I earned a degree as a chartered financial consultant from The American College, in Bryn Mawr, Pennsylvania. That degree was very important to me. Because I always questioned myself and my intelligence, it was important to me to earn a degree in what I do every day—financial advising. In fact, as a reward when I finished, I went out and bought myself a new car.

In elementary school, since I didn't picture myself good in school work, I made it my goal every day to see if I could crack the teacher up and get them to laugh. If I did that I thought, then it was a successful day. Many of the days I was able to accomplish my goal of making the teacher laugh and I was labeled the class clown. Since I was a little disruptive, consequently most of my elementary school years my desk was right next to the teacher.

When I made it to junior high, my studies caught up with me, and I wasn't prepared for the junior high math class. So I was put in a slow math class. Believe it or not, there were actually teachers that made fun of us in the class as well as other students. To make matters worse the "slow" class was way at the end of the hall, and you had to pass all the other classrooms as you went to it. I remember feeling like everyone was watching the dummies go down the hall while all the "normal" kids entered the "normal" classrooms. There was a teacher at the end of the hall in the classroom right next to ours who taught the normal math class. He would stand outside of his doorway with his hands on his hips. As we walked past him, it was very intimidating, and I remember feeling like he was looking at us like we were big losers. He would even make reference to us in his class; when someone didn't get a certain topic, that if they weren't careful, he would "make them go next door with the dummies."

"RIGHT" SIDE OF THE TRACKS

As a result of being in the class, my self-esteem suffered, but I am grateful that I had the experience. In a town of 3,000 there was an unspoken hierarchy from which side of the tracks you lived on, and what your dad did for a living. Everyone knew both of those things about you when they met you. So my dad being a banker and living right next to the country club, everyone knew we were on the "right" side of the tracks. What was interesting was there was no one in the slow math class but me, who was considered to live on the "right" side of the tracks.

This experience made me realize how much people in general are alike. We all have some of the same wants and desires. And if you remember your junior high days, fitting in and being accepted were pretty high up on the list. I think this experience humbled me, and made me realize I was no better or worse than anyone else. Some of the kids in this class became my good friends. I probably would not have taken the opportunity to socialize with them, had it not been for this experience.

I realized how others treated them differently because of their situation. This experience created a desire in me to want to treat others fairly and as equals no matter what their circumstances.

I'm sure if you grew up in a small town this brings back memories. In school we were all classified as a part of a group. And I think society in general is comfortable putting us in a group and is not comfortable if it's not clear where we fit in. When I went on to high school, I kept in contact with some of the kids from our slow math class. We had bonded. I remember sitting with them before school started. As you walked into school, everyone sits in their respective groups. When I would sit with them, my other friends would be curious as to why.

I hated conformity anyway, and hated that others thought they were better just because of where they were in life. I remember being up for homecoming queen, and thinking how surprised some of the kids were about that. I certainly didn't fit the typical "beauty queen." They were even more surprised when I, probably because I had the broadest cross section of friends, won by a popular vote.

Sports came natural to me as I was pretty athletic. Sports are where I excelled, and at the time probably saved me from being a slacker at everything else in my life. At the time, being successful at something helped my self-esteem.

I remember one time in kindergarten, I decided a certain boy in my class was "the" boy that I wanted to "go with." I remember announcing this to my mom when I got home from school one day. The boy's last name concerned my mom as he had many older brothers whose names were often in the paper for various petty crimes and for spending the night in jail. I remember her inquiry as to what on earth made me think that this was the boy to "go with." I informed her that I had challenged all the boys in class to a foot race, and he was the only one who could beat me. I thought that made him pretty cool.

Knowing my mom, she probably rolled her eyes and said, "Oh, brother." I'm sure she wondered what on earth was in store for her with a little girl who picked her boyfriends by the manner I just described.

Looking back on how my life has transpired, I know that I prefer challenges to not being challenged, and I get bored or just don't have fun unless something is challenging to me.

HE BELIEVED IN ME

My father was wise and taught me how to play golf at age five. I started competing in the junior golf program not long after that. I had early success at golf. As you can imagine in the late '60s and early '70s, I didn't have much competition as a girl playing golf in the middle of Kansas. I can't ever remember losing at these junior golf tournaments, and even when they put me with the boys, I often won.

I guess in my little mind I developed this idea that I was really good, since almost no one my age anyway, could beat me.

One of my fondest memories of playing with my dad was when we were at a savings and loan meeting at the Broadmoor in Colorado Springs one summer. Dad had a meeting in the morning and then we had a tee time that afternoon. They paired us with two men my dad did not know from another state.

If you are a golfer, you know that the men's tees are furthest from the hole and so men tee off first, and the ladies tees are forward so women tee off last. As my dad stood on the men's tee box with these two men, they didn't even try to hide how disgusted they were to be paired with a ten-year-old on the golf course, and a girl at that! My dad teed off last and without looking at them as he teed up his ball he said, "Don't worry if she slows us up, I'll make her pick up her ball."

As we drove to my tee box after everyone else had hit, I remember being very nervous feeling pressure to hit a good drive. My dad must have sensed this as he reassured me stating that "I had nothing to worry about." I did hit a good drive, and it was in the fairway, which neither of the men had done. It was also further than the two men and further than the difference in distance between the men's and women's tees.

As I got in on my side of the golf cart, my father laughed and stated "I don't think we will hear anything from them today." I remember how good it felt that he believed in me, when at the time, I didn't have the confidence to believe in myself.

Since I had some success at sports, I would practice often in my two favorite sports, basketball and golf. I would spend hours shooting baskets in our driveway. My dad even put a light out by the goal, so I could practice when it was dark. This didn't please my mom, as she wanted me to be a "well rounded" person, and thought that I spent enough time shooting during daylight hours.

On Saturday mornings when the sun was up, I would play eighteen holes of golf, often with my little brother, and be back home by the time the morning cartoons were on. Often my dad would come home from work in the evening, and we would grab a couple clubs to carry with us and walk across the creek from our house to play a few holes. We would play as many holes as we could, until it was so dark we couldn't see the ball anymore.

Even today, when the sun is setting, and it is considered dusk, I often think of my dad. Especially if I can smell fresh cut grass or hear locust chirping, I think of the times I spent with him. It is funny how a smell or sound can take you back to a certain time in your life.

Even though it is sad to be without him, I'm thankful for the memories and these things that "take me back," so I will never forget.

In Dr. Sylvia Rimm's book *See Jane Win,* her study was done on 1,000 girls who grew up in the '60s and became successful. Many of the girls had similar experiences, but there was one event that they all had independently experienced. It was that someone in their life, when they were slacking off, let them know that they knew they were better than they were acting. In a way, these adults were letting the children know that they believed in them, more than the child was at that time in their life, believing in themselves. I believe this happened to me as well with my father and a few of my teachers and coaches at different times in my life.

THE POWER OF INTENTION

I think that sports can really prepare you for life and for a career. It requires teamwork, goal setting and discipline, all of which are needed to succeed in business. I feel that those attributes help me now in my business. It would be hard to be self-employed without discipline. It would also be hard to run our practice without good teamwork. I am adamant about setting goals for myself, and grew up learning to do that through sports. I remember going to a basketball camp and learning about the power of the mind through psycho cybernetics. The concept of this was a revelation to me. I used this in sports, envisioning the basketball going through the net or the golf ball landing in the cup and hearing the sound that it makes.

To this day, I visualize events before they happen. I practice the positive outcome in my mind to enhance my chances of success in a particular matter. A book I recently read is kind of a psycho cybernetics revisited, *The Power of Intention*, by Dr. Wayne Dyer. Dr. Dyer has read hundreds of books on the psychology, sociology, and spiritual aspects of intention by both modern and ancient scholars.

His research reveals "a fairly common definition of intention as a strong purpose or aim, accompanied by a determination to produce a desired result." Dyer goes on to say "if you are one of those people with a never-give-up attitude combined with an internal picture that propels you toward fulfilling your dreams, you fit this description of someone with intention."

Furthermore, Dyer illustrates these people are "super-achievers and probably proud of their ability to recognize and take advantage of opportunities that arise." Dyer describes people who live at high levels of intention as people who have made themselves available for success. He calls these people "connectors."

To connectors, it all seems so simple: "keep your thoughts on what you intend to create. They perceive seemingly insignificant events as being orchestrated in perfect harmony. To connectors, everything that shows up in their life is there because the power of intention intended it to be."

By thinking positively and focusing on what I intend to have happen in my life, I have been able to accomplish almost everything that I have set out to do.

COLLEGE SCHOLARSHIP

After winning the Kansas state golf tournament my sophomore, junior and senior years, golf "seemed" too easy. So when I graduated from high school, instead of playing golf in college, I accepted a scholarship to play basketball at a junior college. Talk about a challenge, a 5'3 inch tall white point guard?

During my collegiate basketball career, I rarely encountered anyone as short as I was. I loved doing the unexpected, and I averaged 3-5 rebounds a game during my career. Basketball did pay for the first two years of my education, and I was thankful for that. I didn't want my parents to be burdened with the expense, and I didn't want to accumulate debt either.

WE'RE NOT IN KANSAS ANYMORE

After finishing junior college I earned a bachelor degree at Kansas State University. I knew that I wanted to move to an exciting city that would hopefully have more opportunities for a career for me than in a small town in Kansas. I knew two people I could live with in two of the cities that I thought would be exciting and opportunistic, Dallas and Denver. I sent over 100 letters with resumes and followed up with them all by phone. I struck out as not one of the companies was interested in hiring me. This was a very frustrating experience, as I always felt I would be good at something, I just didn't know what.

CHALLENGING MYSELF PHYSICALLY

I ended up with my first job managing a health club that was a national chain at the time. I did this for two years while I fulfilled one of my dreams, which was to try bodybuilding and power lifting. It was the mid '80s and in this area, there were many trainers to pick from and places to get advice and help in competing. I competed only one time in power lifting, and really only because I was working out one day and a power lifting trainer noticed how much I was bench pressing.

He approached me and asked, "Have you ever thought of competing?" I said that I had always wanted to, but didn't know how to train for it. He said he would love to train me at no charge and if I would give him three months he would increase my bench to 250 pounds. So after doing whatever he told me to do, I competed one time in Tyler, Texas. I remembered benching 242.5 lbs. Afterwards everyone wanted to know "who I was." I explained that it was the first time I had competed and probably the last, as I had been dared to do it and to see how much I could do.

I found out later that the state record for my weight class, 148 lbs., was 220 pounds. And the weight I lifted for the bench would have put me second in the nation. My record didn't count because I didn't do the dead lift or squat. I found out later that I could have just done the bar so it would have counted (but I didn't know that at the time). The experience did give me personal satisfaction because I know what I did and it was fun to accept the challenge.

I competed three times in bodybuilding and qualified to attend national competitions. I really had done what I wanted, which was to see how far I could push myself athletically. I also was able to test my will and determination. It is a very grueling and hard sport. Because of the dieting, it isn't just a sport, but a new way of life. I'm thankful for the experience and what it taught me, but I realized at my last competition that I had gone as far as I could go naturally. I wasn't interested in taking drugs to enhance my chances and could tell that the other competitors had. The drugs were easy to get at the time as well.

With the realization of not competing anymore, I knew I needed to get a "real" job and start a career. On a side note, I'd like to share something that for some reason people find interesting about me. When you play the game, "tell the group something that they don't know about you and would be surprised about," besides my being a "homecoming queen," remember the cheesy reality game, that no one wants to admit they ever watched, *American Gladiator*? Well, I was a contestant on the live show, and people seem amused by that.

MY FIRST "REAL" JOB

Back to my career, I received a job doing the payroll for a trucking company, and it was at night from 5:30 p.m. to 3 a.m. I did this for about two years, as I was still searching for what I really wanted to do. A friend at the time was an assistant to Willie Cox, a financial advisor, and I was offered a part time day job as an assistant there, for a man named Ken Comer. I worked from 9 a.m. until 3 p.m. for him and then went to the trucking company to do payroll. This went on for a year. The first week on the job as an assistant, Ken told me he was going on vacation, and he handed me the phone book and said, "See if you can set some appointments for me, for when I get back."

To his amazement, I had several meetings lined up for him when he returned. I think he just gave me the phone book thinking, it wouldn't hurt, but really didn't think I'd set any appointments. He asked me what on earth I had told them, that they wanted to meet with him. I told him that when I called people, I let them know that you were honest and trustworthy, and it would be worth fifteen minutes of their time to see if you could help them, like you have helped other business owners just like them.

I guess this impressed him and he started bugging me about becoming a financial advisor myself.

A PERFECT SCORE

At the time, there was a personality test that was given to potential advisors. The test was supposed to determine, based on your personality, if you would be good as an advisor. The industry believed in the test so strongly that even if you were considered unlikely to succeed, if you did well on the test, you were often hired. After much prodding by Ken, I gave in and took the test. I prayed about God opening or closing a door for me with the results of the test being a sign. Well, it was a fluke. I am sure, as I received a perfect score. So, unwillingly, I might add, I kept my commitment that if I did well, I would "try" it.

So starting with a phone book, a cubicle and an extreme fear of failing, I was determined to make it in this business.

ACHIEVEMENT JUNKIE

Looking back on my life, I realize now that I was an achievement junkie. I just didn't feel good about myself unless I was achieving something. It didn't matter what success I had in the past. I felt like a mouse in a cage on a metal wheel and I couldn't afford to step out of the wheel and stop spinning. I had to achieve something in the here and now to feel good about myself.

It wasn't until this point in my life that I realized the difference in self-confidence and self-esteem. I had one, self-confidence, because of my achievements, but not the other, self-esteem. Fifteen years ago I read a book that changed my life, *The Search for Significance*, by Robert S. McGee. He describes all of the traps we put ourselves in to feel we have self-worth. I was in the achievement trap.

The book goes on to say that the reason we are all equal and have self-worth is because we all have the same opportunity to accept that Christ died for our sins and accepting that fact alone is the reason for our salvation. There is nothing we can do to one up one another or improve on the grace through Christ's death, that has been given to all of us.

THE MOST REWARDING THINGS I HAVE EVER DONE

So knowing that for most of my life I have been an achievement junkie, you might find it interesting that the most rewarding things I have done were not achievements at all. And just as when I interviewed Kay Granger and asked her the most rewarding thing she had ever done, for me, too, it had to do with the people and relationships in my life. When you write "your story" you will most likely find this to be true for you as well.

One of the most rewarding events in my life was the years I had the privilege of helping raise a teenager, Erica Salazar, and help her mature into a young woman.

The other event was when I had the fortunate opportunity to take care of my mother in the last several months of her life as she battled breast cancer. When this experience was over, I felt as if I had lived my whole life for this one task of helping my mom be as comfortable as possible, enjoy her last few months of life on this earth and help her prepare to go from this life to the next.

Witnessing the way she kept her positive attitude, maintained her sense of humor and was so unselfish was a privilege in itself. She made me realize how futile it is to complain about a situation because she graciously accepted where she was and made the best of it. She made me want to make the best of any situation that I might encounter in the future. And if I ever have to cross the horrible bridge of terminal cancer, that if I could have half her courage, half as much of her unselfishness, and half as much of her sense of humor, then I truly will have accomplished something.

If you ever have the opportunity to help someone you care about go through the dying process, do it. I was very apprehensive and it isn't fun by any means, but I'm certain it will be rewarding and you will be glad you did it. (A book that helped me through this process is *Mid Wife For Souls*, by Kathy Kalina.)

MY LIFE SINCE 2004

Well, I left off last time at 2004. There is not a whole lot new in my life since then, but there were a few significant events.

BROOKE MADELINE TURNER

In February of 2006, I had the fortunate opportunity to witness the birth of my niece Brooke. Even my friends who have had children say that they didn't really witness the birth of another human being, as they were a little preoccupied. It was a wonderful experience. I have gotten to see her once a month since she was born, and watch her grow up which has been a huge joy in my life.

UNCONDITIONAL LOVE, BROOKE AND EMILIE

Over the last few years, I have learned unconditional love from two very little people, my niece Brooke and the girl I call my granddaughter, Emilie. The love of a small child that just wants you to pick them up, love on them and play with them is one of the most wonderful things that I have ever experienced in this world. The only thing they really want back, from me anyway, is the exact same thing. When they fall asleep right next to you or on top of you it is like a two-hour hug, one that you really don't want to ever end. I had never experienced this since I have never had children. Sometimes it makes me feel like I have missed something in life by not having children. But I do know I love them as much as I would my own, and they have allowed me to receive a love that I have never felt before. I am thankful to God and them for being in my life, so I could experience the most wonderful form of love I have ever known.

BUSINESS

Along the business side of life, we have formed a partnership within the larger firm that we do our financial advising through. We had a firm create a logo and a branding tagline that expresses how we differentiate ourselves from other firms. You are holding the fourth significant thing that has happened since 2004.

DOROTHY

Lastly, I mentioned before that I had contacted my biological mother twenty years ago. We only wrote through letters so I never talked to her, heard her voice or met her in person. In the fall of 2006 I decided to try to find her again. For some reason, I thought she had probably passed away, maybe due to my own psychology, as I never, even twenty years ago, thought that we would ever meet.

To start the process, as I had done twenty years earlier, I contacted the Kansas Children's Service League where I was put up for adoption. A social worker was assigned to my case and I paid a $150 fee and filled out all that I knew about my mom and submitted the form. Even though I had kept all of her letters, I had lost the envelopes, so I only had her first name, Dorothy, to reference for the search. Of course I had my name and who had adopted me and when.

"ORIGINAL" BIRTH CERTIFICATE

As I read about how to improve your "search" for biological parents, I kept reading that it was advisable to obtain a copy of an "original" birth certificate. This really puzzled me as the certificate I had always had and known looked pretty "original" to me with my correct birth date and other information. I never considered that one was immediately issued when you are born and then changed once you were adopted.

It only took ten days or so to get an original birth certificate sent to me. I was out of town when it arrived so my assistant Allison faxed it to my hotel. My biological mom had signed it and her middle name was Dean, which caught my eye since the father who adopted me had the same middle name. It listed me as "the child." It listed my mom, her mailing address and full name. For my father, it stated "name withheld" and gave his age and occupation but nothing else.

SURPRISED MYSELF

A few weeks after I received the certificate, I received a call from my social worker from the Kansas Children's Service League, the call came while I was at the office. My assistant told me that a woman from Kansas was on the phone for me. It was the end of the day and I wasn't thinking about anything but business. So when I picked up the phone and the woman said her first name and then said, "I think we have found your mother," I was speechless. She had to say hello several times before I could speak and acknowledge that I had heard her. She asked if I was "ok" and I told her I was fine. I was a little shocked and taken aback. I had never had any emotions toward my mother, but now that she was "found" and I thought I might actually meet her, when I got off of the phone, I surprised myself because I cried a little.

STRUCK OUT THE FIRST TIME

I sent the social worker a copy of the birth certificate in case there was any information that might help her. It was a good thing I did as a few weeks later the social worker called and said that based on the information on the birth certificate that I had faxed, the woman they had found was not my mother.

I was a little let down as I thought I had found her and was glad that she was alive. The social worker assured me that this often happens and that they would try again.

Within a month, I received another phone call, and this time they assured me that they had found my mom, and they had confirmed it with the information on my birth certificate. Apparently, when I was adopted in 1963, the Kansas Children's Service League had a policy that they get other contact information of the mother putting the child up for adoption, for example brothers, sisters, or aunts, in case in the future the mother cannot be found. That way there is another contact to try and find her. A letter is sent to these contacts only letting them know that they are looking for a specific individual. They are only asked to confirm if they know where the person is and how to contact them. My mother's sister was the one who responded to the league and let them know that she believed they were looking for her sister, Dorothy. Dorothy's sister gave an address and phone number so the league could contact Dorothy.

The social worker called Dorothy to see if she was open to meeting me. She was and with the new HIPPA laws we both had to sign forms authorizing our privacy and wait for those to be returned. After those were received the social worker made one more phone call asking both of us separately if we were sure we wanted to meet each other. After that was confirmed, we were given each other's addresses and phone numbers and from there, we were on our own.

BEING PREPARED TO MEET HER

It is interesting the events in life that happen that prepare us for the future. In the fall of 2006, before I had the first conversation with my mom, I read *Freakonomics*. I was reading it for business and didn't expect what I found in the book. The author references an adoption study. He mentions that statistically for a person who puts a child up for adoption, advanced education was not encouraged or a part of their life. Likewise, the child didn't have the opportunity for advanced education or it wasn't as expected by their parents. The couple or person who adopts a child statistically grew up in and lived in an environment in which advanced education was expected or more valued.

The book states that as the child grows up, its genes override their environment. Again, statistically, school is hard for an adopted child. This was true for me and also others I have talked to who are adopted as well. As the child matures into a young adult and contemplates what he or she will do in life, the child's environmental influences take over.

The child has friends who are deciding whether to go to college or not and because of the socioeconomic environment they were around with their friends and parents, advanced education is expected and is more the "norm." The child is expected by his or her parents to attend college. They look around and their friends are for the most part all going to college so the child probably does the same and attends college as well. Everyone's situation is different, and this information is on a statistical basis. This was all interesting to me and since I was going to meet my mom, helped prepare me to do so.

OUR FIRST VERBAL CONVERSATION

Dorothy phoned me a few days after we each knew that we had each other's information. At first, it was a little awkward as to "what do you say" in this situation. I had never told her why I chose not to meet her over twenty years ago when we first found each other. So one of the first things I did was to tell her that my mother who raised me had gotten a little insecure about my meeting her, and at the time I didn't feel it was worth hurting her feelings. Besides that, I had done what I had originally wanted to do, which was to thank Dorothy for having me. She was very understanding and said that it didn't matter what my reasoning was that she was sure at the time that I felt I had done the right thing and had a good reason.

I then asked about the son she had told me about from the husband she had at the time. She told me what he did for a living and that he and his wife were expecting their first child and she was very excited about that. She told me that his father, her husband, had passed away five years ago, and she had been alone ever since.

MY PERCEPTION OF "FAMILY"

She also asked me if I had children, which is very natural, and I'm sure she wanted to know if she had any grandchildren. I told her that my perception of family, because of my life experiences, was probably different than most people. I told her I have several children in my life that I am very involved with and who are a big part of my life. I just never "had" any of them. For whatever reason, I have always felt that your family is who you choose it to be. I have my brother and sister and their children, and some close friends and their children who are my family. Besides, I feel I belong in this world because God is my father and we are all related as His children.

We talked about meeting someday in the future and decided to talk again on the phone a week later. We talked a few more times and then set a date in early December of 2006 to meet. You know how time flies and it seemed a long time away, but it quickly came and was here and I then started to prepare myself to meet her. I had told myself that no matter what I found, it had no reflection on who I was as a person. I also wasn't looking for another "family," as I have always believed that my "family" is the one that I was given and raised with and nothing will ever change that. I wanted to understand myself better, but only for that understanding and whatever I found would not make me feel bad about myself. She offered to allow me to stay with her, but I really wasn't comfortable with that as even though she was biologically a part of me, I didn't know her.

As I drove into town contemplating meeting her, I wasn't nervous or anxious outside of being determined not to let anything I found cause me to view myself as a negative reflection of me. It was more of an adventure than anything, and I was excited about what I might learn about myself and what we might have in common.

LOVED AND SECURE BECAUSE OF CHRIST

I had read in *Jesus Life Coach,* by Laura Beth Jones about having a love relationship with God. At the time, I was going through a really low time in my life and after reading about how the author had a relationship with God that when she saw something special, it reminded her God was there. I had prayed about a relationship like that with God and myself. The author talked about how sometimes God seems far away, and so whenever God wanted to remind her that He was around, to show a lady bug to her. She had seen a lady bug land on her windshield that was covered with snow and ice. She had also had a lady bug land on her computer as she was working on her book manuscript inside of a hotel room in New York City.

WHEN I SEE A DIME

When I finished that part of the book, I prayed to God that He seemed far away to me too and that I would like to have that kind of relationship as well. I had read the book *The Power of Intention,* by Robert W. Dyer and read an affirmation one morning that stated, "You are a person who acquires and attracts wealth." After I read that, I was walking my dogs and found a dime on the sidewalk. I thought it was kind of funny as a way for God to tell me He had heard me, but with a sense of humor since a dime is a small way to "start." Because of that and the ten percent we are to tithe, I decided on seeing a dime as my omen. That very day I saw a dime all by itself on the ground. Since then I have seen several dimes isolated and have kept many of them as reminders that God is here and thinks of me.

I bring this up because when I was driving into town realizing I must be getting very close to her house, I wondered if I was doing the right thing. Maybe I was opening a can of worms that didn't need to be opened. I mean "I was put up for adoption for a reason," all of those thoughts were in my head. It is interesting as this is something, meeting her, that I couldn't "not" do, but I did wonder if it was advisable to do it.

Since I arrived early, I needed to run through the drive-through at the bank and I saw a branch of my bank from the road I was on. I pulled in so I could make a deposit and realized I was on the wrong side to use the ATM from my side of the car. I had gone in backwards. I decided it was better to just get out of the car and walk around to use the ATM instead of backing up and pulling around. I got out of the car and as I was walking around, I glanced down by my tire and there was a dime on the ground close to my tire. Now I obviously never would have seen it had I not entered the ATM backwards. I thought this was God's way of making the dime and the situation stand out for me and for me to not question that it was from Him, and a reassurance that everything was going to be ok. I always believed that God had a plan for the home that I was placed in and that everything does happen for a reason, but my emotional side sometimes casts doubt so that I "wonder" about it all.

When I saw the dime, I had to smile: this was the right thing to do and I felt better about my adventure. I phoned my mom to let her know I was in town a little early and if it was ok to come over early. She said it was fine, so that Friday evening, I knocked on her door. She opened it and we met for the first time. We gave each other a short hug and I remember wondering if I would "feel" anything. I didn't. She invited me in and we sat at her kitchen table and proceeded to talk for several hours about everything from what I do now to how she met my father.

MY BIOLOGICAL FATHER

One of the first things I asked of her was how she met my father and what she could remember about him. I also assured her that whatever the circumstances were around their meeting and my being born were ok: it didn't matter, I was just curious to know. Besides, I'm here now, it's not like I can be sent back. I also asked, to make it easier to tell the story, "Would it be a fair statement to say that he probably doesn't know I was born?" She said yes and I then knew there was no point in my ever looking for him. I told myself beforehand that if he didn't know I was born then I would let it go at that.

WHAT WE HAVE IN COMMON

We went out to grab something to eat and to visit some of her friends as she wanted them to meet me. I remember how they all commented on how much we look alike. We have the same striking blue eyes, chin, jawline and smile. The only facial feature that is different is our noses. A friend of hers commented that we both have the same sparkle and wink in our eyes when we smile. I remember looking at her thinking I guess I now have a glimpse of how I will look at 67. When we stood next to each other, our hips met at the same height. She is much shorter than I am so my upper body is longer. She is very small and petite with narrow shoulders. My shoulders are very broad so we don't have that in common.

She has a bubbly and outgoing personality. As we went to all of her regular stops, grocery store, gas station, and so on, everyone seemed to know her name and addressed her by her first name.

POETRY

She shared with me books of poetry that she has written. All of them were about important things or events in her life—her sister, her husband, her son, and even one of her favorite dogs. I was interested because you see I write poetry too and ironically enough I had written a poem about one of my favorite dogs. We laughed about that as we shared our "dog" stories. We spent Friday night, all day Saturday, and Sunday morning together. Before I left, I copied some pictures of her from when she was my age.

It is weird to see someone who looks so much like me, when at 43 I have never known anyone who was biologically related to me. Of course I could have taken after my father, but outside of maybe having his build or frame and shoulders, with the photo of her at my age, we could have been twins.

LIKE A FRIEND I HAD ALWAYS KNOWN

As we said goodbye and gave each other a hug—this time I felt something. It was as if I was hugging an old friend that I had always known. She asked me if I would like to see her again. I told her yes and we decided on another visit in the spring.

As I drove back to Fort Worth, for some reason, I still don't know why, I cried. And it was one of those rare kinds of cries that seemed to last almost the entire trip back. As I was driving, I thought of a poem for her. When I got back I had the poem typed up, framed and sent it to her.

I'm sure we will get together in the spring as we have planned.

Here is the poem that I wrote for her, I hope you enjoy it.

GOD HAD A PLAN FOR YOU AND ME

You and I, we grew a world away, I never dreamed we'd meet someday.

I understand more about me since we've met, and you know I have no regret.

For the way things turned out you see, Is because God had a plan for you and me.

Your beautiful smile, your wink when you laugh, your urge to tell a joke, for that one both of our friends like to poke.

Your caring and giving nature, is what others say about me that they treasure.

Good heart, fun loving and have a good time, and hey we both like to rhyme.

All these things of me are true, which makes me know now, I already knew you.

For God had a plan for you and me, and things have turned out the way they should be.

Thank you Dorothy for having me.

IF YOU OR SOMEONE YOU KNOW IS ADOPTED

Since I wrote *"Tattoo"* and discussed my adoption in that book, I have had people ask me about it. They either have a child who was adopted or are adopted themselves. I do have some advice about it, but I will also say it is a very private and personal decision that everyone needs to decide for themselves.

I know people who have found their parents and one found his or her father in prison, another had children who were adopted because they were abused. It is hard to say what is advisable with any such knowledge or suspicion. If that is the case or suspicion for you, I suggest seeking professional counseling to prepare you for what you may find.

NO EXPECTATIONS

I believe you can't have any expectations of your biological parents wanting a relationship with you. They may or may not. When and if you do contact them, you are in a way interrupting their normal lives, for the time being anyway, and they may or may not want that. I think you need to see it as an adventure only to learn more about yourself, who you are and for that understanding that meeting them can shed light on. Whatever you find is not a personal reflection of you. You are who you are. There probably was a good reason for your being put up for adoption, so consider that as well.

DON'T ASSUME

But also don't assume that your parents don't "want" anything to do with you. They may have not had the financial means they thought necessary to give you what they felt would be a good home and provide for you. They may have truly done it for you. Odds are your biological parents were young and had other adult influences when it came to the decision whether to keep you or not. Let's face it, how many great and perfect (if there is such a thing) decisions did you and I make prior to age 30, especially if we were under a lot of stress.

A GIFT ONLY YOU CAN GIVE THEM

Lastly, when you think about it, if your biological parents have a conscience at all, surely over the years they have thought more than once about their decision to put you up for adoption and wondered, "Did I do the right thing?" You are the only one who can tell them they did and thank them for it. I am not saying they need forgiveness, but they may think they need forgiveness, and in that case, who else but you and God is capable of forgiving them? They could have beaten themselves up, maybe subconsciously all these years. The greatest gift to them just might be for you to meet them and say, "It's ok, I had a great life thanks to your decision."

If this applies to you, I wish you the best on your search.

INFORMATION TO HELP YOUR SEARCH

I am including some of the websites and agencies that may help you in your search, or if you or someone you know is in fact contemplating searching for their biological parents.

- Adoption Registry Connect www.adopteeconnect.com (free site)
- www.ussearch.com
- Adoption Database www.adoptiondatabase.org (free site)
- ISRR www.isrr.net (free site)
- www.searchadoptionrecords.org
- birthfamilyfinders.com

Office of vital statistics for Kansas (785) 296-1400. Most states should have this service for retrieval of statistical birth records. This is where I went to get the original copy of my birth certificate. It was very fast and the fee was only $15 per copy. I was also informed that if they did not have my original certificate that Social and Rehabilitative Services might have it, so that is a second place to check. SRS in Kansas (785) 368-8171.

If your mother was a resident of a Salvation Army maternity home, you may want to check with them at:

Salvation Army Home and Hospital Records, 10 Algonquin Rd., Des Plaines, IL 60016, (847) 294-2090

A.L.M.A. Adoptive Liberty Movement Assn., PO Box 85, Denville, NJ 07834, (973) 586-1358

International Soundex Reunion Registry, PO Box 2312, Carson City, NV 89702, (702) 882-7755

Concerned Unit Birthparents Inc., 2000 Walker St., Des Moines, IA 50317, (515)262-2334

American Adoption Congress, 1000 Connecticut Ave. NW, Ste. 9, Washington, DC 20036, (202) 483-3399

ACKNOWLEDGEMENTS

We all have people in our lives who have made us better than we would have been without their influence. These are those people in my life and this book is dedicated to them.

MY GOD AND SAVIOR JESUS CHRIST

My dad who believed in me before I believed in myself, and my mother who taught me discipline and to care about my reputation and my appearance. You both taught me to work hard and to practice in what I wanted to excel, and that if I did, it would pay off.

Thanks to my brother Barton, because you are eight years younger than me and were a little parrot, repeating everything I said. I was a better person, knowing you looked up to me. To my sister Beth, thanks for being my sister and sharing your kids with me. Rose Turner, thanks for putting up with my brother. You are truly one of the best things that has ever happened to him, and I appreciate you and am glad you are part of our family.

Thank you to my niece and nephews, Amber, David, Kelsey, Jordan and my friends Erica Salazar and her daughter Emilie. You all made me want to be a better person so I could be a good example to you. My grandparents who taught me how to work hard, have fun, love God, and helped inspire me to want to be self-employed and I thank them for it.

Malissa McCracken, thank you for being by my side, being my

friend and believing in me.

Mary Lou Frazier, and the whole Frazier clan, thanks for making me a part of your family and for sharing your love of golf with me.

To my good friend Lewis Runnion, thanks for being support-ive.

Thanks to my friends Nancy Duncan and Terri King for their friendship and letting me stay at their cabin. I started and finished my book at your cabin and what better place for inspiration to write.

To two of my dearest and long time Fort Worth friends Theresa Loving and Karine Moe, thanks for your friendship, for always being able to pick up where we left off and never letting anything get in the way of us being friends.

Carol Glover, thanks for all of your time and interest in my dream. Rhonda Lombardo, you don't know it, but you were the first friend who I felt loved and accepted me, just the way I am. Jamie and Jeff Webb, thanks for putting up with me for seventeen years and for being good friends. Julie (Crane) Mall, Ben Vasconcells and Bruce Snyder, thanks for helping me make it through grade school and junior high. And Sheri Elliott (Garner) and Serena McCall for helping me get through college and Sheri for never giving up on our friendship, even when I wasn't the best friend to you.

My friend and former staff member Allison Hart, thanks for put-ting up with me for seven (for you albeit long) years, thanks for all of your great assistance in growing our firm, you were a big part of our growth and success. I appreciate your friendship too.

Fernandez Cafe (Vickery Blvd., Fort Worth, Texas) thanks for serving such great food and providing a home away from home.

Suzi Hill and Dorothy Wing, thanks for being my friends and going on that cruise. You don't know it, but at the time, it was a low point in my life. I needed friends and I so enjoyed that trip mostly because of you two.

My business partners, James Taylor and Brandon Howard and our staff Sara Archer and Christan Williams for all of the extra help and requests as I finished this book. Thanks to all of you for understanding the time I spent on this dream of mine, and for your hard work in growing our firm.

Trisha Goode for your help in securing quotes for this book and for your help during our staff transition.

Liz Carrington for referring me to the book *Nickel and Dimed*, without it and the inspiration I received from reading it, this book would not be complete.

Austin Garcia, thanks for reminding me of that great line in *Spiderman II, "Spiderman, you and I are not so different."*

Michele McNicol, thanks for encouraging me to write another book and for challenging me on my ideas which made the book even better.

Jan Miller, thanks for keeping me sane!

Howard and Cheryl Hamilton, I appreciate your encouragement and thanks for your feedback and listening. Stacy and Eric Luecker, thanks for your input and encouragement. And Stacy (EssexGraphix. com), thanks for taking my crazy ideas and designing such a great book cover and for all of the hand-holding you have given me during the process of producing this book. Tana Grubb, thanks for all of your great editing and for putting up with my stubbornness and accepting some of my crazy ideas.

My cutting edge study group, Fred Van Patten, Tony Lofaso, Curtis Shinn, Dave Tornetto, Jane Fontaine, Jim Izett and Jorge Vielledent. Thanks for challenging me and making me accountable to my goals. Also, Bill Green for your invaluable advice to us over the years.

My EWGA, NAWIC and BAC families, thanks to you, Fort Worth really is a small town, but in a good way.

My TCC board of directors, which include Joe and Faye Murphy, Sally Proffitt, Lanna Pruit, Virginia Freeman, Rudy Gonzales, Evette Brazille (and unofficially Ricardo Coronado) you all have really helped me be a better advisor to professors and employees of Tarrant County College.

My other board of advisors: Suzi Hill, (and Suzi, thanks for all of your encouragement to get involved in the community; and you probably don't know it, but when we first met, I had picked you as my one and only advisor at the time), Wayne Lawrence and Gail Warrior-Lawrence (you have both pushed me into "out of the box" thinking and challenged me and I appreciate that), John Brancato and Gina Puente-Brancato (thanks for your challenging me as well), JC Cole, Joanna Cloud, John Stone, Ed Turner, Bill and Sherri Rowell, Mike Sweet, Frank and Dawn DeLeo and Steve and Allyson Rahn (unofficially). Thanks to all of you for giving me your honest feedback on how I can improve my practice and telling me when my ideas are a "little too crazy."

Ben Williams thanks for being my first real mentor and for your friendship. Andy Nelson, thanks for helping me feel welcome during my early days at AXA, for putting up with an immature 25 year-old, and for your friendship. Chris Noonan, Jeff Moore and Bob Auer, you are three people who believed in me before I believed in myself! Ken Comer, wherever you are, thanks for making me take that test seventeen years ago. Thanks to John Lefferts for his leadership, vision and desire for us to succeed.

Ricardo Coronado and Victor Puente, thanks for your encouragement, especially to write this section. It was very healing for me to write "my story." Author Kathy Kalina, thanks for your inspiration and for your book *Mid Wife For Souls*, which helped me get through one of the most difficult times in my life.

Pam Minick, thanks for your PR and marketing advice, your encouragement and enthusiasm.

The positive coaches in my life, Mark Frazier, you helped me have fun when I took golf and life too seriously! Ed Church, Jack Heinrichs, Sharon Quinn and Neil Crane, you all helped me have more discipline than I would have had without you. Garret Wheaton, you lead me by your great example, the way you lived your life, with your love for God, and the way you cared about your health.

Jack Lalane, you don't know me, but you were an inspiration to me. When as a kid, I would watch you on a black and white television, you would exercise with things as simple as a chair. You were before your time, and your desire to be fit and healthy made an impact on my life and created a desire in me to do so as well. Carol Burnett, besides great entertainment on many a Saturday night, you taught me how healing it is to laugh, and especially learning to laugh at myself.

And lastly, knowing that our business is a people business, and I decided to write a book about how we treat people and give back to humanity, I knew my team better be able to back up what I had to say about how we value The Human Factor.

So thanks to all of our clients, who challenge us to treat people the way they deserve to be treated and give back to our community.

BIBLIOGRAPHY

INTRODUCTION
Rebecca D. Turner, *Tattoo,* Trafford Publishing, Victoria BC, Canada, 2006

Kate Greenaway, *Mother Goose*, Reed Business Information, Inc., 1987

Thomas L. Friedman, *The World is Flat*, Farrar, Straus and Giroux, New York, NY, 2005

MAKE BELIEVE
Laurie Garrett, *The Coming Plague*, Penguin Group, Inc., New York, NY, 1995, Farrar, Straus and Giroux, 1994

Michael Crichton, *Next*, HarperCollins Publishers, New York, NY, 2006

Malcolm Gladwell, *The Tipping Point, How Little Things can Make a Big Difference*, Back Bay Books/Little, Brown and Company/Time Warner Book Group, New York, 2000, 2002

Stephen D. Levitt and Stephen J. Dubner, *Freakonomics*, Harper Collins Publications, New York, NY, 2005, 2006

Thomas L. Friedman, *The World is Flat*

THE HUMAN FACTOR
Spiderman II, Columbia Tristar Motion Picture Group, Sony Pictures Releasing, 2004

Barbara Ehrenreich, *Nickel and Dimed*, Henry Holt and Company, LLC, New York, NY, 2001

New York Times, The New York Times Company, New York, NY

J.R. Labbe author, Oct. 14th and Oct. 21st, published by *The Star Telegram*

Peter Davis, *If You Came This Way*, John Wiley & Sons, Inc., New York, NY, 1995

THE TEN ATTRIBUTES OF THE HUMAN FACTOR
Douglas McGregor, *Revisited*, John & Wiley Sons, Inc., New York, NY, 2000

Linda Kaplan Thaler and Robin Koval, *Bang*, A currency book published by Doubleday, a Division of Random House, Inc., New York, NY, 2003

Rebecca D. Turner, *Tattoo*

Mihaly Csikszentmihalyi, *Flow: The Psychology of Optimal Experience*, Harper & Row Publishers, Inc., New York, NY, 1990

Edward E. Lawler III, *Treat People Right!*, Jossey-Bass A Wiley Imprint, San Francisco, CA, 2003

Larry Wilson, *Stop Selling and Start Partnering*, John Wiley & Sons, Inc., 1994

Joe Marconi, *Cause Marketing*, Dearborn Trade Publishing, a Kaplan Professional Company, 2002

Richard Earle, *The Art of Cause Marketing*, McGraw-Hill, New York, NY, 2000

Chip Heath and Dan Heath, *Made to Stick*, Random House Publishing Group, a Division of Random House, Inc., New York, NY, 2007

Peter M. Senge, C. Otto Scharmer, Joseph Jaworski, Betty Sue Flowers, *Presence, An Exploration of Profound Change in People, Organizations, and Society*, Bantam Dell Publishing Group, 2005

M. Ray and R. Myers, *Creativity in Business*, Doubleday, a Division of Random House, Inc., New York, NY, 1989

Norman Vincent Peale, *Power of Positive Thinking*, Ballantine Books, a Division of Random House, Inc., New York, NY, 1996

Robert W. Dyer, *The Power of Intention*, Hay House, Inc., Carlsbad, CA, 2004

Ed Horrell, *The Kindness Revolution*, AMACOM a Division of American Management Association, New York, NY, 2006

YOU GET WHAT YOU PAY FOR
Thomas L. Friedman, *The World is Flat*

New York Times

Liza Featherstone, *Selling Women Short*, Basic Books, a member of the Perseus Books Group, New York, NY, 2004

Door County Compass, DesignWise Studios of Door County

HALLOWEEN, RED DYE NO. 2, AND O.J. SIMPSON

Don A. Voorhees, *The Book of Totally Useless Information*, MJF Books in arrangement with Citadel Press, an imprint of Kensington Publishing Corp., 1993

American Idol, produced by Nigel Lythgoe, Ken Warmick, & Simon Fuller, FOX Broadcasting Company

O.J. Simpson, Pablo Fenjves (ghostwriter), Dominick Dunne, The Goldman Family, *If I Did It*, Beaufort Books (Egan Books/ HarperCollins before cancellation), 2007

Thomas L. Friedman, *The World is Flat*

ALL THINGS "RED," ARE NOT CREATED EQUAL

(RED) is a trademark of The Persuaders, LLC and licensed to (RED) Partners

DATA is a multinational non-government organization founded in January 2002 in London by U2's Bono with Bobby Shriver, and activists from the Jubilee 2000 Drop the Debt Campaign

Vanity Fair, Conde Nast Publications

The Independent, Independent News & Media, Canary Wharf, London, UK

GREEN EGGS AND HAM AND OTHER FUN STUFF

Dr. Seuss, *Green Eggs and Ham*, copyright, 1960, Beginner Books a Division of Random House, Inc.: copyright renewed 1988 by Theodor S. Geisel and Audrey S. Geisel, Published in New York by Beginner Books, Inc.

VIRUS

Robert Frost, *The Road Less Traveled,* Touchstone, a Division of Simon & Schuster, Inc., New York, NY, 1980

Door County Compass

Texas Highways, Travel and Information Division of the Texas Department of Transportation

The Fort Worth Star-Telegram, published by the McClatchy Company, Fort Worth, TX

Fort Worth Magazine, Magnolia Media Group, Hurst, TX

The Fort Worth Weekly, Fort Worth Weekly, Fort Worth, TX

Rebecca D. Turner, *Tattoo*

CONCLUSION
Stephen R. Covey, *The 8th Habit: From Effectiveness to Greatness*, Free Press, a Division of Simon & Schuster, Inc., New York, NY, 2004

ABOUT THE AUTHOR
Stephen D. Levitt and Stephen J. Dubner, *Freakonomics*

Laura Beth Jones, *Jesus Life Coach*, Thomas Nelson, Inc., Nashville, TN, 2004

Dr. Robert W. Dyer, *The Power of Intention*, Carlsbad, CA, 2004

Rebecca D. Turner, *Tattoo*

Cause Marketing Awards

"A tangible indicator of a company's commitment to the greater public good is recognition by a respected industry or corporate group that measures the performance of companies against other companies and confers appropriate honors. One such group, the Center for Responsible Business, each year presented its Corporate Conscience Awards. Although the center itself has discontinued its operations, the awards continue under the management of Social Accountability International, a respected human rights organization. These awards honor "outstanding achievements and pioneering programs in environmental stewardship, employee empowerment and diversity, community partnerships, and global ethics."

Categories for which Social Accountability International confers awards for outstanding achievement include:
- Charitable contributions
- Equal opportunity
- Child labor initiatives
- International human rights
- Global ethics
- International commitment
- Education (literacy)
- Animal rights
- Community action
- Responsiveness to employees
- Fair employment
- Family concerns
- Opportunities for people with disabilities

Since this organization began presenting awards in 1987, some of the best-known and most respected names in U.S. and international marketing include:
- General Mills
- Starbucks Coffee

- Avon Products
- Colgate-Palmolive
- British Airways
- British Petroleum
- Economat
- Dollar General Stores
- Novo Nordisk (Denmark)
- J. Sainsbury (UK)
- Wilkhahn Wilkening (Germany)
- W. K. Kellogg Foundation and the Kellogg Company
- Community Pride Food Stores
- Toys "R" Us
- Sporting Goods Manufacturing Association
- Levi Strauss & Company
- Pfizer
- Xerox Corporation
- Shorebank
- S.C. Johnson & Son
- Aveda
- Foldcraft
- Prudential Insurance
- Tom's of Maine
- Time Warner
- Hallmark Cards
- Smith & Hawken
- Ben & Jerry's
- Federal Express
- South Shore Bank
- Johnson & Johnson
- Stoneyfield Farm

Wealth Strategy Advisors
~ *Giving you time for what matters most.*

www.rebeccadturner.com
www.wealthstrategyadvisors.net

**For speaking engagements or to contact the author,
send e-mail to readtattoo@yahoo.com or call 800-283-8946.**

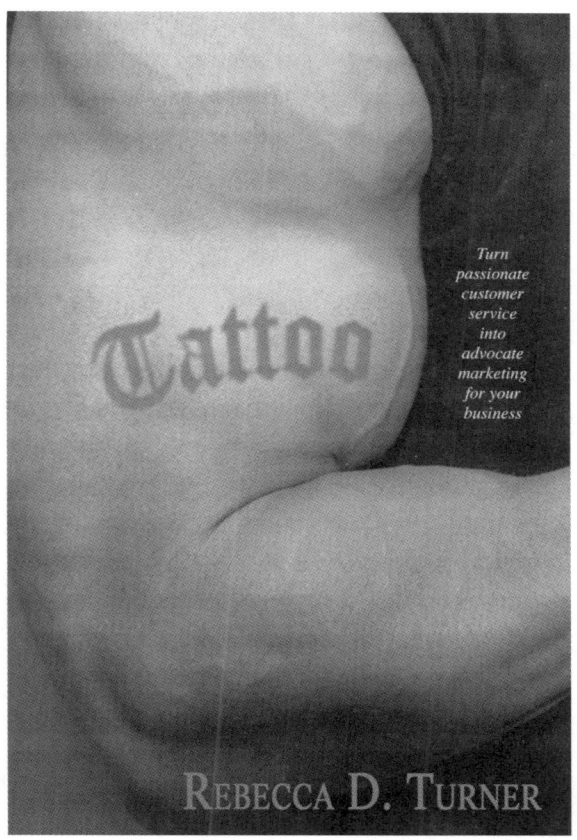

ORDER FORM

To order additional copies of this book, or copies of *Tattoo*,
please visit the respective website
www.readtattoo.com OR www.readvirus.com

Call toll-free 1-800-283-8946
or fill out the order form and fax
817-887-5465
or mail this form and $19.95 + s/h to
Rebecca Turner
801 Cherry St., Suite 2300, Box 34
Fort Worth, TX 76102

(please print)

Name _____

Address _____

City_____ State _____ Zip_____

Phone_____

E-mail_____

Payment method

❏ Check   ❏ Money Order   ❏ Credit Card

❏ VISA   ❏ M/C   ❏ AMEX   ❏ Discover

Credit card number _____

Expiration _____

Name on card (if different from above) _____

Special instructions: